A DICTIONARY of
LIVERPOOL
Ship Portraitists
and Marine Artists

Anthony Tibbles

First published 2023 by
Liverpool University Press
4 Cambridge Street
Liverpool
L69 7ZU

British Library Cataloguing-in-Publication data
A British Library CIP record is available

ISBN 978-1-80207-827-5

Typeset by Carnegie Book Production, Lancaster
Printed in Turkey via Akcent Media Limited

CONTENTS

PREFACE

This work is dedicated to Sam Davidson, who pioneered the study of Liverpool's marine painters and who was a friend, mentor and colleague of mine for many years. Sam was born in 1919 and had a distinguished career as an ear, nose and throat surgeon, and was later Dean of Postgraduate Medical Studies at the University of Liverpool. He was a life-long amateur sailor and yachtsman, and over the years also became a noted expert on the ship portraiture of Liverpool's many marine artists. In retirement he devoted much of his time to researching and writing about these artists and their paintings, advising all the main auction houses and corresponding world-wide with collectors, curators and other experts. He worked closely with the staff of the museums and galleries in Liverpool, and in 1988 was appointed honorary curator of maritime paintings in recognition of his outstanding contribution.

When I arrived at the Maritime Museum in 1986, I knew nothing about the collection of ship portraits and the painters who produced them. The opportunity to get to know more about them came the following year when I helped to develop a permanent gallery to showcase the most interesting paintings in the collection. Sam made a significant input to the project and encouraged and developed my own knowledge of the subject. In 1990 I became head of the curatorial department at the museum and took on responsibility for the collection of paintings, drawings and watercolours.

At that time Sam used to come into the museum at least once a week, principally to use the research facilities of the archives and reading room. Whenever I was free, we always made time to discuss things of mutual interest – the latest enquiries, any forthcoming auctions, potential acquisitions, recent contacts with collectors and dealers or any developments in the research in which we were individually engaged. We would often adjourn at lunchtime to the Athenaeum, the Liverpool club where Sam was a member. There we would have a sandwich, traditionally followed by a chocolate biscuit and a cup of coffee. We were regularly joined by other maritime enthusiasts and the conversation usually returned to one of the subjects we had discussed earlier in the morning.

As part of my curatorial duties I had agreed to prepare a full catalogue of the oil paintings in the museum's collection. The research was spread over nearly a decade as other projects took over, notably the development of the Transatlantic Slavery Gallery which dominated my working life for four years from 1990. After the gallery opened in October 1994, I was able to devote more time to research on the collection, and Sam's advice, comments and knowledge were crucially important. The catalogue was finally published in 1999.

It was during my time working on the catalogue that we noticed several unsigned paintings in the collection that had a number of similar characteristics and appeared to be by the same artist. We were eventually able to identify him as Francis Hustwick, and we went on to produce a publication about him. It is a tribute to Sam's generosity that I was acknowledged as joint author, for although I played a part, the bulk of the research and writing was done by him.

Sam was a significant author in his own right, producing a number of groundbreaking publications. His earliest work, *Maritime Art and Liverpool*, was published in 1986 and was the first comprehensive study of the marine painters who had worked in and around Liverpool from the mid-eighteenth century to the mid-twentieth century. It was a seminal work, identifying a number of artists for the first time, dispelling myths and inaccuracies, and illustrating and listing many of the most important paintings that they had produced. In 1992 Sam published a monograph on Samuel Walters, the most successful of Liverpool's ship portraitists, which also included a comprehensive survey of the work of the artist's father, Miles. This was followed in 2001 by another important volume on the marine painters of the Clyde and in 2005 by an equally important companion volume on the marine painters based in Ulster.

In the decade or so following the publication of *Marine Art and Liverpool* a significant amount of new information about Liverpool marine artists came to light, and many more of their paintings emerged or were identified. There was clearly a case for a second edition. After I had completed my catalogue in 1999, we occasionally discussed the possibility of working together on such a revised and expanded edition, and although I produced an outline proposal and wrote one or two draft entries on artists, we both had other projects on the go and nothing came of the idea.

I retired from the museum in 2009 and moved to Cornwall, and though Sam and I continued to correspond occasionally, sharing the odd snippet of information, my interests and activities were focused elsewhere and I rarely thought about the subject of maritime art.

After Sam died in December 2016 and I was reflecting on our friendship of nearly thirty years, I looked over some of the drafts I had written and realised there was a lot of interesting information. I began to do some additional research and found that a wealth of sources were now available via the internet, and I was gradually sucked in to what has become a major research project. This dictionary is the result.

I have tried to include all the ship portraitists and artists who specialised in marine subjects, whether general shipping scenes or seascapes, both professional and amateur, who lived and worked in Liverpool and Merseyside in the last two and half centuries. I have also included artists in other genres who produced the occasional work on a maritime subject. I have generally excluded landscape artists who might have painted shoreline or coastal scenes. I have also rejected a number of artists who regularly featured local maritime subjects or might have worked for Liverpool shipping companies, such as Kenneth Shoesmith or Arthur Burgess, because they were never resident locally. I have tried to be as comprehensive as possible, so whilst some artists are very well known, a few are known by only a single work.

Each entry begins with a short summary of the artist's career and artistic activity, which is followed by a detailed account of their life, based on as wide a range of sources as possible. There is then a discussion of their artistic output, including the main subjects undertaken, their style and techniques and the range of their work. The entry concludes with brief references to their work in public collections, generally in the UK and North America. A list of published sources follows each entry.

Most entries, but not all, are accompanied by an illustration, generally of a work which is typical of the artist's output. Some of the most important artists have more than one image to show the variety of the work they undertook and the development over their career.

I had originally considered including a list of known works for each artist but, by its nature, the information would never be completely comprehensive or up-to-date. Much information is already available in Sam's *Marine Art and Liverpool*, his *Samuel Walters* and other published catalogues of museums in the UK and USA. The artuk.org website includes the vast majority of paintings in UK public collections. There are also a number of good websites providing details of paintings which have appeared at auction, and whilst full details are often only available on subscription, generally basic details, often including an illustration, can be obtained without charge.

Although I have drawn on Sam's volumes and the published works of other authors, I have started from square one and have checked and confirmed all the biographical information from original sources. I have relied principally on online resources, particularly the genealogical websites ancestry.co.uk and findmypast.co.uk. Through these I have consulted parish and statutory records of births, marriage and deaths, censuses, local directories, military records, probate records and wills, and other records. In order to avoid creating a vast number of footnotes and because these records are so readily available, I have not provided references. I have also made significant use of the British Newspaper Archive, but in these cases I have provided references because they are often far less easy to trace.

In addition to Sam's guidance, I have benefited over the years from discussions and correspondence with a number of museum colleagues, as well as collectors, dealers and maritime historians. These include Michael Charles, Arthur Credland, Dan Finamore, Christopher Foley, H. Crosby Forbes, John Graves, Fritz Gold, David Jenkins, Richard Kelton, Julia Korner, Brian Lavery, Tony Lewis, Dawn Littler, Ian Murphy, Charles Omell, Rina Prentice, Roger Quarm, Stephen Riley, Caroline Roberts, Charles Sachs, Colin Simpson, Michael Stammers, Pieter van der Merwe, Colin White and Paul Winfinsky.

Alison Welsby and her colleagues at Liverpool University Press are always a pleasure to work with and have been unfailingly helpful and efficient. I am also grateful to National Museums Liverpool, especially Laura Pye, Janet Dugdale and Sandra Penketh, particularly for the supply of many of the illustrations, ably organised by Nathan Pendlebury.

Tony Tibbles
Gunnislake, Cornwall
April 2022

ABBREVIATIONS

LCL	Liverpool City Libraries
MM	Mariners' Museum, Newport News, VA
MMM	Merseyside Maritime Museum, Liverpool
NMM	National Maritime Museum, Greenwich
NMW	National Museum of Wales, Cardiff
PEM	Peabody Essex Museum, Salem, MA
RA	Royal Academy, London
TNA	The National Archives, Kew
WAG	Walker Art Gallery, Liverpool
WmAG	Williamson Art Gallery & Museum, Prenton, Wirral

DICTIONARY

John Agnew (1917–1992)

John Agnew was an amateur artist known for a painting of the East Float at Birkenhead which won first prize in the Wirral Spring Exhibition in 1985.

Agnew was born in Birkenhead on 18 July 1917 to James and Mary Agnew (née Duff). His father was killed in France soon after and his mother married William Philip, a greengrocer, in early 1921, when they were living at 415 New Chester Road, Rock Ferry. In 1939 Agnew was living as a lodger at 18 Rock Lane West, Birkenhead, and was working as a chemist in a local soapworks, probably the Unilever factory at Port Sunlight. He married Rita Shaw in 1954. He died on 16 February 1992 when he was living at 95 King's Lane, Bebington.

Unloading Grain, East Float, Birkenhead is an attractive oil painting of a local dockside scene (WmAG).
Lit.: Wright et al. 2006: 60.

James Aitken (1854–1935)

James Aitken was born in Scotland but lived around Merseyside for most of his life. He initially worked as an architectural draughtsman but was established as a landscape and marine painter by his mid-thirties, mainly producing local landscapes, particularly of North Wales, and many seascapes. The seascapes generally feature a wide expanse of sea and a large open sky with small pleasure or coastal craft providing points of interest.

Aitken was born in Newburgh, Fifeshire, in December 1854 to Ann and James Aitken, a master tinsmith and gas fitter. The family moved to the North Meols area of Southport in the late 1850s and in 1861 they were living in Queen Anne Street. By 1871 they were living at 130 William Street, and the 17-year-old Aitken was employed as an apprentice joiner, but this does not seem to have suited him, and in 1881 his occupation is given as architectural draughtsman. He had married Mary Fell the previous year, and they and their 2-month-old son John were living with his parents in what was to become the older Aitkens' family home in Upper Portland Street, North Meols.

By the early 1890s Aitken seems to have successfully made the transition to being a full-time artist. He and his young family were living in Colwyn Bay, North Wales, at the time of the 1891 census and were still there in 1895. He had begun exhibiting at art exhibitions, and in June 1891 the *Liverpool Mercury* reported that he had sold *An Autumn Morning* at the Southport Art Exhibition for £20, a not insignificant sum. The following year he sold two Welsh landscapes at the same show for similar amounts, and in September that year he was awarded 10 guineas and a gold medal for the best work of art exhibited at the National Eisteddfod. When his younger brother died in 1894, the *Liverpool Mercury* described Aitken as 'a well-known painter of Welsh landscapes'.[1]

By 1901 he had moved back to the Mersey, living at 28 St Vincent Road, Egremont, where he was still living in 1911. On this later occasion his occupation is given as 'artist, landscape and marine' and many of his seascapes date from around this period. He seems to have moved to the Isle of Man soon afterwards and was certainly there by 1918, though he continued to exhibit at exhibitions in Merseyside. He also entered work for all the major regional art academies and the RA, where his *Off the Welsh Coast* drew the attention of the *Liverpool Daily Post*. 'A mackerel sky and what the old Greek poet described as "the innumerable laughter of waves" are drawn and coloured in the lighter medium to excellent decorative ends.'[2] It is a description that could characterise much of his marine work.

Aitken was highly regarded in his own time and was a member of the Liverpool and Royal Cambrian Academies. He died at Gullane, Port St Mary, on the Isle of Man on 22 March 1935 and left £829. His son John Ernest Aitken (1881–1957) and daughter Gladys May Aitken (born 1894) were also landscape artists.

There are few examples of his work in public collections but there are typical examples in MMM and WAG. His paintings often come up at auction in the UK.

Lit.: Wright et al. 2006: 61; Tibbles 1999: 25–26.

---

1 *Liverpool Mercury*, 23 June 1891; *Liverpool Mercury*, 24 May 1892; *Manchester Courier and Lancashire General Advertiser*, 9 September 1892; *Liverpool Mercury*, 30 October 1894.
2 *Liverpool Daily Post*, 6 May 1918.

James Aitken, *Entrance to the Mersey at Flood Tide*, signed, c. 1895, 67 x 97 cm. Much of Aitken's output focuses on the sea and sky rather than the vessels portrayed, as in this typically atmospheric canvas. (NML/MMM)

Samuel Austen, *Black Rock Fort and Lighthouse*, c. 1830, 53 x 88 cm. The fort and lighthouse at the entrance to the Mersey regularly feature in ship portraits and other views of the river. (NML/WAG)

Samuel Austin (1796–1834)

Samuel Austin was a watercolour artist, specialising in landscapes and maritime scenes. He was secretary of the Liverpool Academy.

Austin was born on 30 September 1796, the son of Samuel and Mary Austin. He was baptised on 23 October 1796 at the Wesleyan Chapel in Mount Pleasant, Liverpool. In 1806 his mother, probably a widow by then, entered him for the Blue Coat School. In 1809 he became a clerk to William Barber, a merchant, but left to pursue a career as an artist. He probably spent his early twenties in London where he is said to have had lessons from Peter de Wint (1784–1849). He exhibited at the RA in 1820 and probably on 29 June that year he married Elizabeth Sophia Adams at St Mary's Lambeth. They were living in Great Nelson Street, Liverpool, when he exhibited at the Academy in 1822. A son and daughter were both baptised at St Peter's Church on 27 January 1824, followed by two other daughters in June 1831 and March 1833. On each occasion Austin was listed as an artist living in Russell Street, and the same address is given in the street directories from 1823 to 1834.

In addition to selling paintings, Austin made a living principally from teaching and taking private pupils. He was a member of several artistic societies and exhibited regularly in Liverpool and London from 1820. He exhibited at the Liverpool Academy between 1822 and 1832, becoming a member in 1824 and serving as secretary from that same year until 1830. He was a founder member of the Society of British Artists in 1824 and became an Associate of the Society of Painters in Watercolour in 1827 and a full member in 1834. He was awarded a prize of £15 by the Society for the Encouragement of the Fine Arts for 'professional merit' in 1831.[1]

Judging by his surviving work, Austin seems to have travelled fairly extensively, including visits to France, Germany and the Netherlands, and he was probably on a sketching trip when he died at Cefn-y-Gribin, near Llanfyllin, Montgomeryshire, on 15 July 1834.

Austin worked principally in watercolour, producing landscapes and maritime-related scenes. The latter were usually coastal views and the subjects include *Unloading the Catch*, *Grey Horse on a Seashore with Fishermen*, *Figures on a Shore*, *Looking Out to Sea* and *Clearing the Buoy*. In his later years he painted a small number of oils, including *Bootle Landmarks* and *The Black Rock Fort and Lighthouse, Liverpool* (WAG), a *View of the Lune* (Lancaster City Museum) and two views of the waterfront at Southampton (Southampton City Art Gallery). In 1834 his directory entry lists him as a portrait painter but no works of this nature have come to light.

Lit.: Davidson 1986: 125–26; Bennett 1978: 29–30; *ODNB*; Morris and Roberts 1998: 52–53; Wright et al. 2006: 75.

———

1   *Gore's General Advertiser*, 18 August 1831.

James Bell, *R M S Atlantic*, signed, 33 x 27 cm. RMS *Atlantic* was wrecked off Halifax, Nova Scotia, in 1873. This was painted retrospectively for one of the seamen who survived. (ARTUK/ NML/MMM)

James Bell (active 1890s–1900s)

James Bell was almost certainly a Liverpool-based mariner who was a part-time artist. Unusually he painted on small sheets of milk glass and his portraits follow a standard format with only slight variation.

The information that Bell was a seafarer comes from descendants of fellow shipmates with whom he served on SS *Karina* and SS *Politician* and for whom he produced paintings of those vessels.[1] Although he was listed in *Gore's Directory* in 1905 as a 'marine artist' living at 1 Lander Road, Litherland, in north Bootle, neither he nor any associated family were there in the 1901 or 1911 censuses, and it has not been possible to find any more details about him from this or other sources. There are a number of seafarers by the name of James Bell listed in crew lists of the period, but none can be identified as the artist with sufficient certainty.

Each of his paintings follows a similar layout, with a profile view of the vessel at sea within a lifebelt, and the vessel's name at the top and the port of registration at the bottom. A masthead with appropriate house flag is placed diagonally behind the lifebelt and sprays of flowers are fed into the grab rope. A number of paintings also show a ribbon attached to the grab rope with the legend 'MIZPAH'. This is a favourite Victorian tag, often attached to jewellery, which can be roughly translated as 'I will watch over thee.' It is Hebrew in origin and features in the biblical story of Jacob and Laban. By the late nineteenth century it was associated with tokens of affection or items used as a talisman of protection for those facing separation. Sailors could be very superstitious and it was probably the latter connotation that was intended here. At least two of the paintings were painted for Bell's shipmates and it may well be that, given their modest nature, fellow sailors were his principal market.

The majority of the known paintings are of vessels sailing from either Liverpool or Cardiff, though examples of vessels from other ports such as London, Sunderland and even Antwerp are known. The paintings are not dated, but approximate dates can be gauged from the vessels depicted and it is possible to date a few works to within a year or two. A painting of SS *Gallia* can be dated between November 1898 and early 1899 and one of SS *Moranmore* between 1899 and 1901. In at least one case, that of a painting of RMS *Atlantic*, which was lost in 1871, it appears to have been completed long afterwards, the 'Mizpah' ribbon perhaps associating it with a survivor of what was a major disaster in which over 500 passengers lost their lives, though only 10 of the 141 members of the crew died.

There are several examples of Bell's work in both MMM and NMW.

Lit.: Tibbles 1999: 27–28; Wright et al. 2006: 96.

---

1   Information from donors of two paintings, MMM, collection files.

W. J. J. C. Bond (1833–1926)

William Joseph Julius Caesar Bond was a landscape and marine artist, who was particularly influenced by the work of J. M. W. Turner. He had a long and prolific career and his paintings were highly regarded by contemporaries. He is represented in a number of public collections and his work is still regularly seen in the salerooms.

Bond was born on 22 August 1833 to William Bond, a schoolmaster of Knotty Ash, and his wife Susannah. He was baptised William Joseph at St Mary's RC Church, Highfield Road, on 1 September, and his uncle Edward stood as godfather. When the census was taken in 1841 his father was still at the school at Knotty Ash, and three older sisters and a younger sister are also listed. Sometime after this Bond was sent away to school at Stonyhurst College in north Lancashire, and when he returned he was apprenticed to Thomas Griffiths, a miniature painter and restorer, with the aim of learning the trade of picture restoration and cleaning. As he himself recalled some years later, he 'began sketching a little out of doors and Mr John Miller happening to see some of my work advised me to follow it up entirely and I have done so ever since'.[1]

Bond had probably already begun painting when the census was taken in 1851, when he was living with his mother and his siblings in Richmond Row. His father is not mentioned and his mother's status is given as married, and she describes herself as a broker. No occupation is given for Bond. He began exhibiting at the Liverpool Academy in 1853, becoming an Associate in 1856 and a member in 1859.[2] He also exhibited at the British Institution in 1859.

At some point during the 1850s Bond moved to North Wales, and he was living in Bangor when he married Jane Douglas Ellis, the daughter of an ironmonger from Caernarvon, in the Anglican Cathedral there on 12 May 1860. It was perhaps an odd choice – he had been born and brought up a Catholic and she had been baptised at the Moriah Calvinist Methodist Chapel in Caernarvon. In 1861 they were living in Llanberis along with her father, Owen Ellis, a 69-year-old widower. Bond is described as a landscape painter. Two daughters and a son were born in North Wales between 1862 and 1867.

They were back in Liverpool by 1868, living in West Derby Street. Jane's father was still living with them there in 1871 and they were employing a general servant. Bond is again listed as a landscape painter. During this period, he was regularly exhibiting at the Liverpool Autumn Exhibitions and at Suffolk Street and the RA.[3] He was a member of the Liverpool Society of Watercolour Artists and exhibited there in 1882. He was also offering private lessons in 'oil painting and watercolour drawing'.[4] From the 1870s he had a studio in South Castle Street.

Despite prospering professionally, the censuses in 1881 and 1891 show that Bond and his wife were living apart. He remained in Liverpool, probably living with his stepmother and then later with his widowed sister Marion, an embroideress. His wife had returned to Wales, living with two unmarried daughters first in Llanberis and then in Colwyn Bay. She died in Penmaenmawr in March 1895.

By 1896 Bond had moved to Hoylake, and in 1901 he was living with his unmarried daughter Margaret in Massey Park, Liscard. He is listed as a widower and landscape painter. Ten years later they were still living there. At some point in the next decade or so he moved to Queen's Avenue, Freshfield, near Formby, where he died on 29 March 1926. Probate was granted to a retired clerk and retired art dealer in the sum of £1,983.

Bond was influenced by several contemporary local landscape artists, including William Davis, J. W. Oakes, Robert Tonge and William Huggins. It is interesting to note that an art dealer and his clerk passed off a copy of one of Bond's paintings as a work by Tonge to a Birkenhead collector, and they were only exposed when the unfortunate buyer happened to see the Bond original in another dealer's showroom.[5] However, Bond's

---

1   Bennett 1978: 43.
2   He exhibited at the Liverpool Academy, 1853–67.
3   He exhibited at the Liverpool Autumn Exhibitions 1871–1901, Suffolk Street 1860–70 and the RA in 1871 and 1874.
4   *Liverpool Mercury*, 6 January 1870.
5   *Liverpool Mercury*, 5 April, 16 May 1887. The culprits were sentenced to four months and two months.

W. J. J. C. Bond, *The Beach at Scheveningen*, signed and dated 1878, 92 x 153 cm. Bond's marine works are mainly coastal scenes, often with vessels pulled up on the shore as well as in the water, as here. (ARTUK/NML/WAG)

greatest influence was J. M. W. Turner, and on occasions he imitated Turner's work quite closely. Much of his work is of landscapes, but he also produced a large number of maritime scenes. In general, they depict coastal activities along the shore and in estuaries, rather than views at sea. There are evocative views of locations around the Mersey and also on the North Wales coast, including the castles of Conway and Caernarvon from the sea. Other works show ships at anchor or vessels making for the harbour, and have titles such as *Homeward Bound*.

When and how Bond acquired his additional names is not clear, and he appears only as William Joseph in all official records. He almost always signed his work 'WJJC Bond' with his initials in a monogram.

He is well represented by both oils and watercolours in the collections of WAG, WmAG and in some other public collections.

Lit.: Bennett 1978: 43–45; Davidson 1986: 126; Morris and Roberts 1998: 86–87; Tibbles 1999: 28–29; Wright et al. 2006: 105–06.

Edwin Brown (1845–1936)

Edwin Brown was a Liverpool chemist who enjoyed painting as a pastime, and later, in retirement, produced some competent marine works. He is probably best known as the father of Samuel J. M. Brown (q.v.), one of the leading professional maritime artists of the early twentieth century.

Brown was born in Leicester on 17 February 1845, the son of Joseph Brown, a model maker, and his wife Mary, a milliner. By 1861, aged 16, he was apprenticed to Daniel Hendry, a chemist and druggist, in Great Homer Street, Liverpool. He married Amelia Elizabeth Best at Trinity Chapel, Wavertree, on 4 January 1871 and the census for that year confirms his occupation as a druggist and informs us that they were living at 49 Everton Brow. According to family information, Brown had a deep interest in the sea and made several voyages as a pharmacist and ship's doctor. It seems probable that these were undertaken in the 1860s before he married and began a family. The censuses for 1881 to 1901 record his growing family of a son and four daughters. They also show that they lived at two addresses in Brownlow Hill and were sufficiently successful to employ a general domestic servant. Brown's wife died in February 1904. Three of his children married, Catherine in 1903, Samuel in 1905 and Amy in 1907. By 1911, when he and his two unmarried daughters were still living at 211 Brownlow Hill, he had taken on the role of running a post office in addition to his occupation as a chemist and druggist. His elder daughter, Mary, was assisting with the postal work and his other daughter, Jane, was acting as housekeeper.

Mary died on Christmas Day 1919, and in late 1920 Brown decided to retire to Caerwys, in North Wales, principally for the sake of Jane's health, which had had never been good. Sadly, she died in March 1921, but he continued with the move, and in June when the census was taken he was living there with Mary Wells, described as his 'adopted daughter', and her sister, Christina. Brown died there on 22 February 1936, leaving £3,132.

Davidson states that several 'highly competent marine paintings' remained in the family in 1986 and comments that Brown had 'great potential' and could 'have made his mark as a marine painter'. No works seem to have passed through any auctions or sales in recent years.

Lit.: Davidson 1986: 114.

Samuel J. M. Brown (1873–1963)

Sam Brown was one of the most successful marine artists of his generation, producing posters and other promotional material for many of the leading shipping companies in Liverpool. He also produced attractive watercolours, many of which were sold as inexpensive reproductions and became very popular.

Samuel John Milton Brown was born in Wavertree, Liverpool, on 13 April 1873 to Edwin Brown (q.v.) and his wife Amelia. In an interview later in life he commented that his father 'spent hours painting pictures although it was not his job to do so, and he made me want to paint'.[1] He was educated at Liverpool College and was apprenticed to a firm of lithographers at the age of 14. He was fascinated by ships and spent most of his free time around the Pier Head and the docks, and according to family accounts he made several voyages to sea. He also took classes at Liverpool School of Art under the direction of John Finnie (1829–1907), an engraver and landscape artist.

In 1901, aged 27, Brown was working as a freelance lithographic artist, and as a single man he was still living at home in Brownlow Hill. He married Annie Beatrice Derbyshire in the spring of 1905 and they moved across the Mersey, where their son Edwin was born in 1907. In 1911, when Brown described himself as a marine artist, the family were living at 16 Tancred Road, Liscard. At this time he had a studio in Moorfields, but later moved to premises in St Anne Street which were approached through a sugar-importing yard.

For many years after the First World War the family lived in Belgrave Street, Wallasey. Brown's wife died in early 1933 and eighteen months later he married Gladys

---

1   Davidson 1986: 114.

Samuel Brown, *The Pride of the Port*, signed, 75 x 124 cm. This large watercolour, featuring RMS *Mauretania* off the Liverpool waterfront, was probably commissioned by Cunard for an advertising poster when she entered service in November 1907. (Bonhams)

Gwendoline Horrox, some twenty years his junior. On the death of his father in 1936, they moved into the paternal home Bodlondeb, in Chapel Street, Caerwys. By this time Brown's eyesight was failing, but he continued to paint, though his subject matter tended to reflect the countryside near to his new home. In the 1939 register, Samuel, Gladys and Edwin had been joined in their Caerwys house by Gladys's widowed mother, Emily, and her sister, Mabel.

In 1953 the family moved to a smaller and more manageable house at 28 Alwyn Gardens, Upton-on-Chester. Brown died in the Deva Hospital in Chester on 4 January 1963, leaving £3,421 in his will.

Over the course of more than fifty years, Sam Brown undertook work for many shipping companies and produced the usual posters and promotional literature for them, but he also completed a range of other commissions. His preference for working in watercolour no doubt meant that his work was more modestly priced and available to a wider public than that of some of his contemporaries. He was adept at producing smaller-scale paintings, often of sailing ships and other small

vessels battling against the elements. In 1912, in conjunction with the *Liverpool Daily Post and Mercury*, he produced the first of his 'Magic of the Mersey' series, a set of six coloured prints, priced at 2s.6d. This proved very popular and a second set was published in 1913.

Brown's early observations and sea-going experience gave him a great knowledge of the technical features and structures of the vessels portrayed, and he had a gift for inventing an attractive composition. This is well illustrated in his large masterly watercolour of 1908, *The Pride of the Port*, which shows the *Aquitania* off the Pier Head.

He exhibited at the Autumn Exhibitions at the Walker Art Gallery and served as secretary of the Liverpool Sketching Club for many years, being later elected as a life member. He was a member of the Liverpool Academy and from 1937 of the Royal Cambrian Society, serving as its president from 1958 to 1960.

A number of museums and libraries hold examples of his work, including MMM, WmAG and LCL.

Lit.: Davidson 1986: 114–16, 124.

Joseph Butler (1787–c. 1865)

Joseph Butler appears in various official records, including some local directories, as an artist, but is known from only a handful of works. He probably took up painting seriously after he retired as a plumber, glazier and metalworker in about 1850.

Butler was almost certainly born in Liverpool on 26 November 1787 and baptised at St Nicholas's on 14 January 1788, the son of James, a tin plate worker, and his wife Mary, who lived in College Lane. He married Ann Brown from Manchester at St Ann's, Liverpool, on 24 October 1813, when he was also working as a tin plater. He is listed as a plumber in Haworth Street, Everton, in *Gore's Directory* of 1839, though the 1841 census describes him as an ironmonger, aged 50, living with his wife Ann, aged 45, and their nine children.[1]

Butler seems to have retired about 1851 when *Gore's Directory* lists him as an artist living at 9 Meadows Street, and his eldest son, also Joseph, had taken over the plumbing business in Everton. It seems he was not at home when the census was taken in March 1851, as only his 56-year-old wife Ann was living at this address with three of their daughters. Ann is described as an 'artist's wife', and when their daughter Charlotte married in April that same year, her father's occupation was also given as artist.

Butler appears in the directories from 1855 to 1859 and again in 1864 as a 'marine and landscape artist', by then living at 25 Albert Street, Paddington. In the census of 1861, he and his wife are living at 27 Albert Street, though his occupation is again given as plumber. The only other clear references to him are in September 1861 when 'Isabella Norrish, youngest daughter of Mr Joseph Butler, artist of this town' died, and in June 1863 when 'aged 70, Ann, wife of Mr Joseph Butler, artist of this town' died.[2] No record of his own death has been located.

Little of his artistic work has come to light. There is a lithograph *George's Dock Basin and the vicinity of St Nicholas* produced by Day & Co. and published by 'Thomas Hardman from a drawing by Joseph Butler'. From internal evidence the drawing dates from 1852 or later, and shows the busy scene on the Liverpool waterfront. Another lithograph by T. Picken, *Panoramic View of Liverpool from the Mersey*, from an original in the possession of Daniel Scott, 'the Town by J. Butler, Shipping by S. Walters', was published in Liverpool by William Thomson in 1853. An unsigned oil painting on panel depicting the same view, which might have been the original for the lithograph, appeared at auction in the early 1980s. The only other known work is a watercolour in WmAG entitled 'View of the original Monk's Ferry A.D. 1163, sketch by J. Butler, author Panoramic View of Liverpool 1853'. The Liverpool Record Office has a print by W. G. Herdman of Everton Brow 'after a drawing by Joseph Butler'.

Lit.: Davidson 1986: 126–27.

---

1 Ages are rounded down to the nearest multiple of 5 in this census.

2 *Liverpool Mercury*, 23 September 1861, 23 June 1863.

Benjamin Carrier (1862–1915)

Ben Carrier was a ship's steward who in later life was also a very good part-time ship portraitist.

It seems that Carrier was born Benjamin Alexander Caraher in 1862, the alternative spelling being used by the family in the 1850s and early 1860s. He was the son of Scottish-born James Caraher, a ship's steward, and his wife Margaret, who had married in 1853, and were then living in Lodge Lane. He was baptised on 22 June 1862 at St Michael's in the Hamlet, Toxteth. His mother died in 1869, and in 1871 Ben and his older twin brothers, Samuel and Joseph, were living as boarders with Robert and Hannah Hughes in Eastham Village, suggesting that his father was at sea. By the 1881 census James had remarried. Then a chief ship's steward, he was at home at 45 Rosalind Street, Kirkdale, and his wife's name is given as Jane. Carrier was living with them and, following in his father's footsteps, is listed as an 18-year-old ship's steward.

From surviving crew lists we know that Carrier served on the Booth Line's *Anselm* in 1883 and on the Cunarder *Campania* in 1898. He made a number of voyages as chief steward on the Canadian Shipping Company's smaller *Lake Champlain* and *Lake Erie* in 1902/3 and the final record is for a voyage on the Pacific Steam Navigation Company's TSS *Orcoma* in 1913.

On 22 June 1884 Carrier married Marion Alice Gill at St Mary's, Walton-on-the-Hill. In each of the next three censuses he was obviously at sea, as Marion is listed as the head of the household with a growing family. They moved from Bootle to Seaforth in the 1890s and were living at 40 Caradoc Road in 1901 and 146 Sandy Road in 1911. Ben Carrier died in the autumn of 1915, aged 53.

In terms of paintings, two portraits of Elder Dempster's *Tarquah* survive from 1905, and in 1910 he painted the *Orcoma*, on which he served.

Lit.: Davidson 1986: 128.

Joseph Chatham (1849–1881)

This watercolour artist is known only from a handful of works completed in the two years before he died in 1881 at the age of 31. John Joseph Chatham was baptised in St Michael's Roman Catholic Church in Limerick on 1 August 1849, the son of John Chatham and his wife Margaret. His father was a seafarer and gained his master's certificate in 1852, having been at sea since the age of 13.

The family moved initially to Dublin and sometime after 1855 to Liverpool. Nothing else is known of John's seafaring career, and by 1861 he was dead, the census listing his wife as a widow of 35, with her son Joseph, 12, and two daughters. They were living at 134 Vauxhall Road and she was working as a stewardess. Ten years later, although Margaret was still working as a stewardess and her daughters were employed as dressmakers, they were living in a court in Brook Street, near Princes Dock, which suggests that their circumstances were fairly poor. Although Chatham was now 21, no employment is listed for him.

By 1881 Chatham was trying to make a living as a marine artist, the occupation given in the census and also in *Gore's Directory* for the same year. He was unmarried and was living with his mother, then retired, and sister, Elizabeth, at 7 Tooke Street, Everton. Unfortunately, within six months he was dead, being buried in Ford Roman Catholic Cemetery on 13 August 1881.

His surviving watercolours show him as a competent artist. There are a group of four small watercolours of steamships, signed and dated to 1880 or 1881, in the collections of MMM.

Lit.: Davidson 1986: 128.

John Woodman Cobb (1916–1988)

John Woodman Cobb was a draughtsman at shipbuilders Cammell Laird in Birkenhead. He produced illustrations for many of the company's brochures and is also known for a small number of ship portraits.

Cobb was born in Birkenhead on 25 November 1916, the son of William Cobb, an engineer patternmaker, and his wife Annie, whose maiden name supplied his middle name. He served in the Merchant Navy during the Second World War, making his first voyage as a junior engineer on the New Zealand Shipping Company's *Rangitiki* in September 1939. At the end of the voyage in January 1940, his discharge papers tell us that he was 5 feet 10 inches tall, had grey eyes, brown hair, a fair complexion and a scar on his right ankle. After the war he worked as a draughtsman for Cammell Laird, where he also undertook illustrations and drawings for many of the company's brochures and publicity material. He married Hilda Cutler in Birkenhead in early 1944. He died on 14 June 1988.

Cobb is mainly known for just two ship portraits now in WmAG – both are very colourful with accurate detail and they are shown as typical profiles at sea.

J. W. Cobb, *R M S Windsor Castle*, signed, 88 x 165 cm. Cobb's training as a draughtsman ensures a very accurate and detailed portrait of the liner. (WmAG)

Charles Cockerham, *Pier Head, 1908*, signed and dated 1908, 79 x 132 cm. This is one of Cockerham's most ambitious canvases, showing the variety of activity around the Liverpool waterfront. (NML/MMM)

Charles Cockerham (1870–1951)

Charles Edward Cockerham seems to have had some very limited seafaring experience before joining his father as an estate agent. From his teenage years he indulged his passion for marine painting, although he never established an artistic reputation, and on the evidence of his surviving works his talents were modest.

Cockerham was born in the spring of 1870 in Southport, the son of Edward Turner Cockerham and his wife Eliza. The 1871 census shows that Edward Cockerham had originally come from Leeds and was working as a bookkeeper, though by 1881 he was in partnership with his brother-in-law, Charles Padley, in a firm of estate agents. The family was living with Padley at 73 Oriel Road, Bootle, and Edward and Eliza seem to have inherited the house and business when Padley died in 1883.

In 1891, when he was 20, Cockerham was still living with his parents and his occupation is given as an accountant. However, it seems he had some seafaring experience as a young man. Davidson learned that he had been to sea on sailing ships and had also worked in Harland and Wolff's shipyard. He obtained the information from the artist Keith Griffin (q.v.), who visited the older man as a 14-year-old in 1941.[1]

Cockerham married Mabel Murphy, the daughter of a chief steward, in 1894, and by 1901 they were living in Curzon Road, Waterloo. By this time he had joined his father in the family estate agents' business, but that clearly did not satisfy him as he additionally described himself as 'a marine artist'. To what extent he was able to devote himself to artistic activity is not clear, but he is listed as a marine artist in the local directories from 1902 until 1935. One of the most bizarre references to him is an advertisement which appeared in the *Bolton Evening News*, and no doubt other papers, in which 'Mr Cockerham, Ship's Portrait Painter, 9 Union Court, Castle Street, Liverpool' recommends Dr Tibbles Vi-Cocoa as 'a stimulating refreshing drink'![2]

Cockerham's father died in 1907, and by 1911 he and Mabel were living at West View, Handfield Road, Waterloo. He was still practising as an estate agent, as a stamped address for 'Cockerham & Knight, estate agents, 37 Oriel Road and 3 Chapel Street' appears on the census return. He also lists himself as 'artist, steamship and yacht specialist / designer of saloons, deck houses etc.' In 1921 he was boarding with a family at 16 Oriel Road, Bootle, and his wife was living with relatives in Wallasey, which she continued to do for the rest of her life.

Cockerham produced paintings throughout his life, and a sheet of surviving business notepaper, probably dating from the 1930s, claims that his business was established in 1886 and that he was a 'steamship, airship and yacht specialist'. He probably did not sell very many works. When Griffin visited him in 1941 his bedsit cum studio at the top of some apartments was crammed with marine paintings, ship models and other related material.

Cockerham died on 20 May 1951 in Westminster House Home for Elderly People, aged 81, though his permanent address was given as 17 Norma Road, Waterloo. He left £597 in his will.

Only about a dozen paintings are known, mainly in MMM and the Ulster Folk and Transport Museum, Belfast. They include several standard portraits of steamers and a couple of more accomplished works of vessels in subdued and atmospheric light. Paintings of yachts and sailing vessels have also passed through the market in recent years. His atmospheric view of the Pier Head, Liverpool, dating from 1908 and now in the MMM, is perhaps his most impressive canvas.

Lit.: Davidson 1986: 128; Wright et al. 2006: 249; Tibbles 1999: 69–70.

---

1   Griffin had recently had his first drawing published and received the invitation from Cockerham as a result.

2   *Bolton Evening News*, 8 October 1900.

C. Arthur Cox (1858–1941)

Arthur Cox was a full-time artist, principally of marine scenes. Although he achieved some success in his lifetime, it is unlikely that he was able to sustain a living from painting, and he probably relied on support from his cotton broker family until the turn of the century. Thereafter he seems to have lived in more straitened circumstances.

Charles Arthur Cox was born in Liverpool on 13 December 1858, the second son of Charles Hudson Cox (q.v.), cotton broker and amateur artist, and his wife Eliza. The family had moved to 17 Church Road, Claughton, outside Birkenhead by 1861, and were in nearby Shrewsbury Road in 1871. On the latter occasion they were employing a housekeeper and two other general servants.

When the census was taken in 1881, Arthur was 24, and was staying with the Revd Arthur Wright, rector of Tilston, Cheshire. He described his occupation as 'artist painter'. He exhibited regularly at the Liverpool Society of Painters in Watercolours in the 1880s and 1890s and served on the hanging committee in 1890 and was elected secretary in 1894.[1] In 1891, he was living in the family home in Shrewsbury Road, Claughton, with three of his unmarried sisters and an aunt, Lucy Cox. He is described as 'artist to *The Graphic*', the illustrated weekly magazine established in 1867. Interestingly, although Cox was the only male member of the household, he is not listed as the head, but as 'son', indicating that they still regarded his father, Charles Hudson Cox, who by this time was living in Texas, as fulfilling that role. Could this perhaps indicate that they expected him to return or even that they were unaware that he had emigrated permanently. They were clearly an unusual family – although Cox's eldest sister Ada described herself as 'housekeeper', Edith was a 'society lady' and Gertrude a 'retired chicken farmer'!

By 1901 the house in Shrewsbury Road seems to have been sold and the family had gone their separate ways. Cox was now living with his cousin Clement Cox, a general broker, and his family in Handfield Road, Waterloo.

He is listed as an artist, living on his own account. Ten years later his circumstances had further deteriorated, and he was boarding with Tinniswood Robertson, a freight clerk, and his wife in Hawthorn Cottage, Bridge Road, Poulton. As usual, his occupation is given as artist.

The next reference to Cox is in 1939 when he was living with Richard A. Lewty, a dental surgeon, and his wife in Sutton Coldfield, Warwickshire, and his occupation is now given as 'retired artist'. It has not been established whether Lewty was a relative, but another cousin, Louisa E. A. Cox, who is described as 'incapacitated', was living at the same address. Cox died in nearby Solihull, aged 82, in the spring of 1941.

Initially Cox's work was received with some caution. The *Liverpool Mercury* described a view of *Duke Street, Liverpool* as 'very well drawn but faulty in colour', taking particular issue with a house coloured red.[2] Later his *Morning on the Atlantic* was praised by the same paper – 'the action of the water being treated with much skill'.[3] He seems to have regularly sold his work at the exhibitions of the Liverpool Watercolour Society, including a view of *Birkenhead by the Mersey* for 12 guineas and *Low Tide* and *Sunset by the Mersey* for 6 guineas each.[4] In 1894 he was awarded a prize of $50 and a gold medal for a seascape at the Cotton Palace Exhibition, Waco, Texas, where his father lived.[5]

There a few of views of the Mersey in public collections, including *Wallasey Pool and a View of Wallasey*, dated 1875 (WmAG), and the *Old Salt Warehouse, Liverpool*, in the Weaver Hall Museum and Workhouse, Northwich. Cox's works occasionally appear on the market, usually marine-related scenes, such as an *Isle of Man Steamer*, dated 1901, *On the Mersey – Sunset Glow*, or a watercolour entitled *Homeward Bound*. He exhibited occasionally in the Walker's Autumn Exhibition, including *Straits of Belle Isle at Sunrise*, which the *Glasgow Herald* compared to the work of the more famous marine artist Henry Moore (1831–95).[6] There are a number of illustrations

---

1   *Liverpool Mercury*, 3 April 1890; *Liverpool Mercury*, 22 January 1894.

2   *Liverpool Mercury*, 11 May 1881.
3   *Liverpool Mercury*, 12 February 1894.
4   *Liverpool Mercury*, 31 May 1886, 16 May 1892.
5   *Liverpool Mercury*, 21 December 1894.
6   *Glasgow Herald*, 29 May 1895.

C. Arthur Cox, *Wallasey Pool*, signed and dated 1875, 23 x 40 cm. Cox shows a model boat race in the tidal inlet of Wallasey Pool with the town of Wallasey in the background. (WmAG)

in *The Graphic* during the period 1881–93 and there is a poster for *Bearings – The Cycle Magazine*, dating from 1895–96 in the Smithsonian American Art Museum.[1]

Lit.: Davidson 1986: 130; Wright et al. 2006: 273.

---

1   The poster is signed 'Arthur Cox', but the museum assumes that Charles Hudson Cox and Charles Arthur Cox are the same person.

Charles Hudson Cox (1829–1901)

Charles Hudson Cox was a Liverpool cotton broker who was an amateur artist and exhibited marine subjects at many exhibitions. He emigrated to Texas at the age of 60 and thereafter mainly produced watercolours of the local flora and pastoral subjects.

Cox was born in Liverpool on 28 January 1829, the son of Edward Cox, a broker, and his wife Maria, of Soho Street, Islington. The family had moved to Park Road, Toxteth, by 1841, but Charles and his brother John were staying in St Peter Port, Guernsey, with Edmund Ricks, a schoolmaster, presumably being educated. He was back living at the family home in Park Road in 1851 and was working as a clerk in his father's firm, and by 1853 he had progressed to brokering, along with his father and elder brother, Edward.

In April 1854 Cox married Eliza Hutchinson Lomax in Llangollen, and by 1861 they had moved to 17 Church Road, Claughton, and had two sons and a daughter. Eliza died in 1870, and Cox was living at Forestlands, Shrewsbury Road, Claughton by 1871, with three sons and three daughters. Although he was staying with a fellow broker, John Pilkington, in Wavertree on the night of the 1881 census, four of his children were at home in Shrewsbury Road. On all three occasions he is described as a cotton broker.

In 1889 Cox emigrated to Texas and settled in Waco. The surprising move to the United States might have been encouraged by the example of his eldest son, Edward, who had emigrated some years earlier and had established a brokerage business in Galveston. Cox became seriously ill in 1901 and was recommended to take a trip to the mountains of Colorado, where he died on 7 August 1901. He was buried in Oakland Cemetery, Waco.

Cox was an amateur artist and produced mainly marine-related subjects. He exhibited approximately fifty works in exhibitions across the country between 1866 and 1889. Few are now known, but they include a view of the Alfred Dock, Birkenhead, signed and dated 1879, and a view at sea entitled *A Thousand Miles from Land*. Once he had established himself in Texas, Cox's interest turned to watercolours, and he was inspired by the landscape around him, in particular the hillsides and wild flowers of the Bosque Valley. A typical work is entitled *Springtime in Texas in Buffalo Cover* (1893). He received a gold medal at the Cotton Palace Exhibition in Waco for the best portrait in oil in the amateur competition in 1894.[1] The McCulloch House Museum in Waco has a collection of 20 of his paintings. There do not appear to be any examples of his work in British public collections.

Lit.: Davidson 1986: 129–30.

_____

1 *Liverpool Mercury*, 21 December 1894.

Henry Dawson (1811–1878)

Henry Dawson is well known as a landscape and marine artist. He spent just over four years in Liverpool in the 1840s, though few of his works can be attributed to this period and none of his marine paintings are obviously of local scenes.

Dawson was born in Hull on 3 April 1811, the son of a cheesemonger and a flax dresser, but his family returned to their native Nottingham in the following year, where he was to remain for the next thirty years. He initially worked in the lace industry, but began painting at an early age and became a full-time artist in 1835. He received some lessons from W. H. Pyne (1769–1843) in London in 1838, but was otherwise self-taught.

Dawson married Elizabeth Whittle in June 1840, and they were living with his widowed mother in Nottingham in 1841. Six months after his mother's death in February 1844 they moved to Liverpool, where he lived at 19 Ashton Street, Pembroke Place. Although he had no local contacts, his work soon attracted attention from dealers and collectors and he made friends with several local artists, including Philip Wescott (1815–78) and Richard Ansdell (1815–85). He took some further lessons at the Liverpool Academy from Dr Rowland, becoming an Associate in 1846 and a full

Henry Dawson, *H M S Victory*, 61 x 91 cm. Many of Dawson's marine canvases use lighting to dramatic effect, none more so than this 1850s view of one of the most iconic vessels of all time. (ARTUK/NML/LLAG)

member in 1847. He exhibited *View on the Mersey* at the Academy in October 1846.[1] In an attempt to further his career, Dawson moved to London in 1849, living initially in Croydon before moving to Camberwell and then Chiswick. He retained non-resident membership of the Liverpool Academy until 1852, when he ceased to exhibit.

Dawson struggled to make a name for himself in the capital, but he found patrons in the Midlands and the North of England, and in the last year of his life he received a boost to his reputation with an exhibition of more than fifty of his works in Nottingham.

Dawson died on 13 December 1878 in Chiswick and left just under £7,000. His son, Henry Thomas Dawson

(1841–c. 1896), was also a marine artist and his second son, Alfred (1843–1931), was an engraver and lithographic artist. Alfred's son Montague (1890–1973) became one of the most famous marine artists of the twentieth century.

Henry Dawson's marine scenes show the influence of Turner and are generally very atmospheric and often set at sunset. The emphasis is on the overall composition rather than the individual vessels, which are often generic and not identified.

He is represented in many of the major regional art galleries, including Lady Lever Art Gallery and WAG, but in surprisingly few maritime museums, perhaps because his works are viewed principally as seascapes rather than for their maritime content.

Lit.: *ODNB*; Bennett 1978: 90–91; Wright et al. 2006: 295.

---

1   *Liverpool Mercury*, 2 October 1846.

GEORGE PEABODY YARMOUTH. N.S.

Aristides de Clerck, *George Peabody, Yarmouth, N.S.*, 41 x 56 cm. The artist showed little interest in the niceties of atmosphere or perspective and used strong, bold colours to produce simple portraits which appealed to his fellow seafarers. (Courtesy of the Peabody Essex Museum)

Aristidius de Clerck (1841–1899)

Aristidius Amatus Joannes de Clerck, a former seafarer from Antwerp, was a prolific ship portraitist in watercolour and spent four or five years in Liverpool in the mid-1870s.

De Clerck was born in Ostend, Belgium, on 22 September 1841, the son of Joannes Petrus Clerck and Fedelia Lencke. He spent his early years at sea and married Virginia Maria Caterina Scheltiens, an Antwerp innkeeper, in 1869, coming ashore shortly afterwards and beginning his career as a painter. Their daughter Virginia Maria was born in Antwerp in 1870, but by the time their son Joannes Petrus was born in the autumn of 1872 they had moved to Liverpool.[1] A second son, Josephus Aristidius, was born on 18 March 1875 when they were living at 33 Brasenose Road, Kirkdale, but he died on 10 May 1876, by which time the family had moved to 1 Snowdon Street, Vauxhall. Another daughter, Maria Godileve, was born on 11 September 1877 when the family had moved again, this time to 88 Luther Street, Everton. De Clerck gave his profession as 'marine artist' on all the birth and death certificates. He is also listed as a 'marine painter' in *Gore's Directories* between 1874 and 1878.

De Clerck and his family returned to Antwerp at some time after 1877 and two further children were born there in 1881 and 1889. He continued his career, producing portraits of visiting ships, particularly of vessels from the countries of Scandinavia. He died in 1899.

De Clerck worked in watercolour, often with gouache and ink to add extra detail, a medium which allowed him to work extremely fast and produce works very quickly. This meant that he was able to sell his work at very modest prices; for instance, in 1875 he sold two paintings for £1.10s each and a third, in a frame, cost £2.7s.6d. – less than half the price of many other contemporary ship portraitists.[2] During his early artistic career, including the time he was in Liverpool, he sought to emulate the work of his more expensive competitors, but after he returned to Antwerp he increasingly simplified his paintings, using broad areas of bold, bright colour, most reminiscent of folk art.

There are examples of his work in museums in Scandinavia and North America. A pair of oil paintings of Yarmouth-owned barques, signed and dated 'A de Clerk Liverpool 1874', are in the Yarmouth County Museum, Nova Scotia, Canada, and a number of other Liverpool period works are in private collections.

An exhibition of de Clerck's work was held at the Maine Maritime Museum, Bath, from May 1992 to January 1993.

Lit.: Davidson 1986: 99, 109; Martin 1992.

---

1 Exact details cannot be ascertained as the certificated entry of birth is damaged.

2 Martin 1992: 11.

Thomas Dove (1812–1886)

A native of Whitby, Thomas Dove was an accomplished marine painter but seems to have harboured an ambition to be an academic artist. However, he was obviously a realist, and having also trained as a house painter, he practised a dual career on Merseyside for many years. His later years seem to have been subject to some misfortune, and returning to Whitby, he died in destitution.

Little is known of Dove's early life in Whitby. He was born in 1812, probably on the east side of the Old Town, and as a youth he was apprenticed to George Croft, a house painter with a shop in the National School-house Yard. Benezit reports that he was a pupil of George Chambers Senior, who was working in Widow Irwin's house- and ship-painting business, before leaving for London in the early 1820s.[1] Some of Dove's early paintings show the influence of Chambers and he seems to have spent a month with Chambers in London in the late 1820s. By 1833 he was resident in Liverpool, where on 27 April he married Susannah Bolton, also a native of Whitby, at St Peter's Church. He described himself as an unspecified 'painter', the same description used to describe him when their first child was baptised in April 1834. When their daughter was baptised in the following June, and they were living in Nelson Street, his occupation is given as 'marine painter'. However, in *Gore's Directories* he is also listed under 'Painters, Plumbers and Glaziers' (marine) between 1835 and 1847, which suggests that he had supplementary employment in these years.

By 1841 Dove and his wife were living in Duncan Street, and had a family of three sons and two daughters, aged from seven to seven months. He described himself as a 'marine painter', a term used in all subsequent censuses. He exhibited at the Autumn Exhibitions at the Walker Art Gallery on five occasions from 1840 until 1851, and at the Liverpool Academy in the latter year. In 1844 and 1846 the family was living in Park Street, Toxteth. By 1851 they had moved to Pool Road, Liscard; three of the children had died and two others had been born. They were living at the same address in 1861 with all their children and Susannah's widowed mother, Alice Bolton, who was 79.

Although Dove was seemingly well known to local ship owners and captains and 'possessed of ability', he struggled as an artist and, as a later writer reported, he was 'overshadowed by the late Samuel Walters'.[2] His personal circumstances seem to have deteriorated in the late 1860s, and he and his wife appear to have separated. In 1871 he was living on his own in Laurel Road, Tranmere, and his wife was living in Sheffield with their oldest daughter, Alice, and her husband Joseph Sanderson, a provisions dealer. Interestingly, she describes herself as 'artist's wife'. She continued to live with the Sandersons until her death in 1892. A print of a self-portrait of Thomas Dove, which probably dates from around this time, survives in the Whitby Museum and shows a rather sad-looking and introspective man.

It seems that Dove had always maintained his links with Whitby, and in September 1867 the *Whitby Gazette* carried an article about a painting he had recently completely in the town, and commented that he made 'occasional visits' to the place of his birth. In the words of the newspaper, the painting in question, *Launching the Lifeboat*, 'combines a vivid transcript of local scenery with an event of genuine interest'. It goes on to describe the composition and concludes

> We are not learned in the jargon of art criticism, and we certainly have no wish to use extravagant terms of commendation, but to us, the picture appears to possess very great merit, both in composition and execution. The sea and sky are exceedingly well painted, and, altogether, "Launching the Lifeboat" presents a formidable description of what those who dwell in Whitby have too often seen – a storm at sea. We understand the painting will be sent to the next exhibition of the Royal Academy.[3]

---

1   His association with Chambers is also confirmed in his obituary, *Whitby Gazette*, 25 December 1886.

2   *Liverpool Mercury*, 18 December 1886.
3   *Whitby Gazette*, 21 September 1867.

Thomas Dove, *Combatant Entering the Mersey*, signed and dated 1837, 69 x 116 cm. This early work of the ship-rigged *Combatant* in two views off the north Wirral coast is one of Dove's most accomplished and attractive paintings. (ARTUK/NML/MMM)

Thomas Dove, *West Derby off Egremont*, signed and dated 1861, 71 x 117 cm. A late work typical of
Dove's mature style, demonstrating his attention to detail with the careful depiction of the smaller
vessels in the background. (ARTUK/NML/MMM)

According to his obituary in the same paper, not long after this painting was completed Dove decided to return to Whitby permanently. He was 'employed in drawing portraits of iron screw steamers, the first notable picture of this sort being one showing the launch of Whitby's first steamer, the *Whitehall*, in June 1871.[1] This painting is now in the Whitby Museum, and though full of charming local detail, it does not have the elegance and bravura of some of his earlier works. He clearly kept some connections with his family in and around Liverpool, and in the 1881 census he was staying in Birkenhead with his daughter-in-law Mary Jane, the wife of his son Thomas, who as a mariner was away at sea.

The *Whitby Gazette* obituary continues Dove's story. Although his 'pictures sold well for a time, his commissions being many and lucrative', as he grew old 'infirmities crept upon him, his hand lost its cunning and … he sank into poverty'. A proposal to start a public subscription was unsuccessful, due 'in no small part to his own laxity', and in late 1885 he was persuaded to enter the Union Workhouse, where 'he was allowed a separate apartment, where he amused himself by painting, reading etc.'[2] Dove died on 22 December 1886 at the age of 74 and was buried in St Mary's Cemetery.

His Liverpool obituarist perhaps summed up the situation best in writing that he was 'of kindly disposition and very unassuming manners, but, in addition to his eyesight failing him, he was deficient in energy and push for the times'.[3]

At his best, Dove is a fine artist, producing canvases that are comparable with those of Samuel Walters. He tends to avoid a standard ship portrait, but features a very accurate portrayal of the vessel, often in the middle ground with plenty of other activity in the vicinity and set against a familiar but detailed location. There are relatively few surviving works by him, but there are good examples in the Whitby Museum, MMM and the New Brunswick Museum, Canada. One of his most impressive canvases is a large and comprehensive panorama of the Liverpool waterfront, which has a wide variety of shipping in the river, including screw steamers, paddle steamers and sailing vessels, against a detailed view from Princes Dock to Albert Dock, and prominently featuring the dock warehouses, St Nicholas's Parish Church, the Tower, Custom House and other landmarks in the town.[4]

Lit.: Davidson 1986: 72–76, 88; Morris and Roberts 1998: 202; Tibbles 1999: 76–78; Wright et al. 2006: 306.

---

1   *Whitby Gazette*, 25 December 1886.
2   *Whitby Gazette*, 25 December 1886.
3   *Liverpool Mercury*, 31 December 1886.
4   'The Port of Liverpool', sold at Sotheby's, London, 13 November 2012, lot 107.

Gordon Ellis (1920–1978)

Gordon Ellis was brought up on Merseyside and studied naval architecture. He became a full-time painter in 1948, completing many shipping company commissions in his early years, but he later extended his work to include historical subjects, hunting scenes and portraits of children. Although Ellis spent virtually all his adult life away from the area, the Mersey and its ships provided much of the inspiration for his marine subjects, and many of his paintings were sold locally.

Many authorities state that Ellis was born in 1921 and died in 1979. In fact, Ian Gordon Ellis was born in Warrington on 17 July 1920 and died on 3 December 1978. His father, Aytoun Ellis (1896–1966), who was a part-time writer and historian, had served as a lieutenant in the Scottish Rifles and was later a travelling medical representative. Ellis was educated at Merchant Taylors' School in Crosby, where the art master, Claude L. Fisher, encouraged his interests and talent. In his spare time he drew ships, and he had a special pass from the Dock Board to be able to visit the docks. After leaving school, he worked briefly in the studio of the Liverpool Printing Works, where Walter Thomas (q.v.) was the chief artist. Ellis was already an accomplished artist, and two of his paintings were illustrated in *The Tatler* as early as March 1938. In September 1939 the family was living in Harrogate, and Ellis had begun his apprenticeship as a naval architect. During the Second World War he worked in the design department of John Brown's shipyard on Clydebank.

In 1948 Ellis made the difficult decision to become a full-time painter, and he was fortunate that at this period many shipping companies still regarded it as important to acquire a painting of each new vessel they had built. Ellis secured a number of such commissions, and by 1958 it was reported that his pictures could be found all over the world 'in Scandinavia, Belgium, Spain, Portugal, Greece, Germany, United States of America, Australia and South Africa'.[1]

Ellis married Barbara Kay in 1945, and from the late 1940s they and their family lived at the White House, Lowick, near Berwick-on-Tweed. He maintained his strong connections with Merseyside, not only in terms of his subject matter, but through the circumstance that the majority of his works were sold by Frederick Boydell at the Boydell Galleries in Castle Street, Liverpool. In November 1968 the gallery held an exhibition of Ellis's marine paintings, and it continued to sell his limited edition prints for many years after his death from a heart attack in December 1978.

Ellis was a talented and versatile artist, and Davidson includes a comprehensive account of his approach to painting and the careful research he undertook, particularly when completing major commissions such as his large canvas of the training ship HMS *Conway* on the Mersey, which was commissioned for the assembly hall of the school at Plas Newydd, Anglesey, in 1963.

He is represented in a number of public collections, including museums in Merseyside, Kirkcaldy and in the Science Museum, London.

Lit.: Davidson 1986: 120–24; Tibbles 1999: 79–80.

---

1   *Berwick Advertiser*, 14 August 1958.

Gordon Ellis, *Centaur in the Tropics*, signed, 51 x 76 cm. This is one of Ellis's earlier works, a typical profile portrait, enlivened by a dramatic sky. (ARTUK/NML/MMM)

Parker Greenwood, *Germanic in the Mersey*, signed and dated 1886, 40 x 66 cm. This is typical of Greenwood's moody portraits. (NML/MMM)

Parker Greenwood (1849–1904)

Parker Greenwood was a seasoned mariner, who left the sea in his mid-thirties and became a successful marine artist.

Greenwood was born in Liverpool on 26 March 1849 at 5 Court, Wright Street, Toxteth Park. He shared his unusual first name with his father and grandfather, who were both masons, and his mother was Bridget Ellen Greenwood, previously Robinson, née Kelly. There is no documentary support for the suggestion in many later sources that his first forename was George, and this name does not appear on his birth certificate. This notion probably springs from a confusion with a carver, gilder and photographic artist of that name who worked in Liverpool in 1867. By 1851 his father had died, and the rest of the family, comprising his mother, Ellen, her daughter by an earlier marriage, an older brother and older sister, were living in straitened circumstances at 2 Bruce Street, Toxteth Park. His mother's occupation is given as laundress, but she is also listed as a 'parish recipient', indicating that she was receiving charitable support to look after her family. She remarried in July 1853, though her new husband, John Wynne, was absent from the 1861 census, and Ellen and her Greenwood children were living as lodgers with a policeman and his family at 1 Orphan Street. Ellen was still working as a laundress.

Greenwood's seafaring career is partially documented in a number of surviving crew lists, and though he probably went to sea as a teenager, the earliest voyages noted are in 1869 when he made passages on *W Fairburn* and *Virginia*. He was no doubt at sea when the 1871 census was taken, and next appears when he married Elizabeth Murphy, a blacksmith's daughter, on 19 June 1878 at St Silas's, Liverpool, when his occupation is given as 'sailor'. He was at home for the 1881 census when he and his wife were living at 2 Meaburn Street, Islington, with their infant son Robert. Greenwood is described as a 'mariner' and crew lists survive for a number of voyages for Cunard in 1882 and 1883. He made at least four voyages on *Gallia* and two on *Bothnia*, and though he failed to join the ship on one occasion and was reported as deserting in New York on another, they continued to employ him. He is listed as an able seaman earning £4 a month. His occupation was also given as mariner when his second son, Thomas, was born in October 1885 and they were living at 33 Whitefield Terrace, Everton.

Greenwood probably left the sea when his wife died in the summer of 1889. With two young sons to bring up he needed to be at home, and painting no doubt offered a potential career. He was already a very competent artist, as his earliest surviving canvas of *A Cunarder in a Storm*, dated 1880, shows. In the 1891 census when he was living at 145 Berry Street, Bootle, he described himself as a 'marine artist' and he is similarly described in local directory entries in 1892, 1894 and 1895. By 1901, when his eldest son had left home, he was living at 36 Church Street and was listed as an artist. He died on 13 December 1904 at 13 Rimrose Road, Bootle.

Greenwood's attractive ship portraits are set around the wider Liverpool approaches, often in the Mersey itself, and include the general activity on the river, with ferries, flats and small craft going about their business. He often chose to set his scenes at sunset and bathes the scene with a golden light, as in *Shipping in the Mersey* (MMM), one of his last works, and one of the most impressive. There are other good examples in the MMM, WmAG and NMM.

Lit.: Davidson 1986: 105–07, 111; Wright et al. 2006: 379; Tibbles 1999: 82–89.

K. A. GRIFFIN

Keith Griffin (1927–2007)

Keith Alistair Griffin was one of the most prolific and successful marine artists working on Merseyside in the second half of the twentieth century.

Griffin was born in Manchester on 11 March 1927, but was brought up and educated on the Wirral. In 1939 he was living at 12 Red House Bank, West Kirby, with his father Robert, a dock gateman, his mother Gwendoline, and three siblings. About this time he was attending Hoylake Parade School. His artistic skills were recognised as a young teenager when two of his drawings, a galleon and a Bristol Beaufighter aircraft, featured in the pages of the *Liverpool Echo*.[1] He served in the army in the final year of the Second World War and then studied at the Laird School of Art, Birkenhead. In 1955 he married Barbara E. Sutton and they had two daughters. From 1967 he worked as a commercial artist, but his real interest was always in maritime subjects. He undertook some commissions for portraits of new ships for companies such as Blue Funnel, but the majority of his work featured historical subjects. These included famous vessels such at CSS *Alabama* and HMS *Bounty*, and a variety of sailing ships, yachts and other vessels. Many of these paintings were reproduced as prints. He died in March 2007, aged 80.

The only public galleries with works by Griffin are WmAG, which has a portrait of the Liverpool Bar Lightship and a view of the bridge of a sailing vessel, and MMM which includes a former Blue Funnel commission of the cargo liner *Priam* (1966). Exhibitions of his work were held at WmAG in 1984 and 1992.

1   *Liverpool Echo*, 19 April 1941, 21 March 1942.

Lit.: Davidson 1986: 128; Tibbles 1999: 90.

Keith Griffin, *Priam at Sea*, signed, 67 x 92 cm. This portrait was commissioned by the ship's owners, the Ocean Steam Ship Company, in 1966. (ARTUK/NML/MMM)

John Hall (1836/37–1887)

John Hall was a Scottish-born naval architect and painter, who spent most of his adult life in Liverpool and who increasingly became known as a marine artist. Although few of his works are now known, he was well respected in his own lifetime.

Almost nothing is known of his origins and early life, and he first appears in the local directories as a naval architect living at 15 Cleveland Square, Toxteth Park, in 1865. By 1871, when he first appeared in the census, he was living at 48 Carter Street with his wife Mary and two children, George who was 5 and Helen, 2. His age is given as 34 and his place of birth as Scotland. Unfortunately, with such a common name and lack of detail, it is not possible to establish his origins with any certainty. The family seems to have spent a period in Ireland, as his daughter was born there in 1868/69, and this might also explain why Hall is not listed in the directories between 1866 and 1869. He was sufficiently successful financially for the family to employ a young girl as a general domestic servant.

The census lists him as a naval architect, an occupation confirmed in directory entries between 1870 and 1876. It seems, however, that his activities as an artist were developing, and from 1877 until his death the directories style him as 'marine artist and naval architect'.

By 1881 the family had moved to 89 Moscow Drive, West Derby, and his occupation now only cites 'marine artist/painter', perhaps indicating that he now regarded this as his main activity. According to the *Liverpool Mercury* he died suddenly at 4 Normanby Street aged 50 on 14 May 1877.[1]

A couple of months later, the memorial fund committee of the Artists' Club issued a circular letter to its members seeking support for the family of the 'late John Hall, marine painter'. The *Liverpool Mercury* reported that this had resulted in the promise of 'pictures and drawings from artists in the metropolis, as well as from resident and other Lancashire practitioners'. The paper went on to praise the 'straightforwardness and sterling qualities of the deceased artist'.[2] Four years later in 1891, the census seems to indicate that the family was surviving without undue hardship. His widow, Mary, was living at 26 South Road, Waterloo, as a fancy goods dealer. Her two children were living at home, she was employing a live-in assistant in her business and she also had a young local girl to undertake the general domestic duties.

Perhaps surprisingly for an artist who seems to have been so well regarded in his own lifetime, very few works by Hall have been identified or come to attention. There are single examples in the Merseyside Maritime Museum and the India Office Library, London, but there is better representation in Yarmouth Museum and New Brunswick Museum in Canada, and Davidson notes a number in private collections.

In addition to working in oils, Hall seems to have been a competent watercolourist. A few ship portraits are known in this medium, and after his death the *Liverpool Mercury* noted that he had submitted three works to the Liverpool Society of Painters in Watercolours exhibition at the Walker Art Gallery. The 'most characteristic' was *Craft in the River* which featured a group of river flats 'carefully drawn' and showed the 'artist's true feeling for the aspect of the originals in their everyday use'. The writer commented that 'It was in coastal scenes, and such drawings as the above that the deceased was seen at his best.' The other two works were named as *Deganwy Village* and *Mouth of the Conway*, suggesting that Hall might have undertaken a wider variety of subjects than previously thought.[3]

Lit.: Davidson 1986: 107, 111; Wright et al. 2006: 386.

---

1   *Liverpool Mercury*, 17 May 1887.

2   *Liverpool Mercury*, 18 July 1877.
3   *Liverpool Mercury*, 4 June 1887.

John Hall, *Alexander Yeats*, 61 x 107 cm. This fine portrait with a detailed view of the vessel shows Hall at his most accomplished. (New Brunswick Museum – Musée du Nouveau-Brunswick, http://www. nbm-mnb.ca, 1960.9)

Joseph Heard (1800–1859)

After Samuel Walters, Joseph Heard was probably the most talented and successful ship portrait artist working in Liverpool in the nineteenth century. He was also one of the few who seems to have been able to make a living from his artistic skills alone, and it is perhaps significant that he described himself as 'artist' rather than 'painter' on almost all formal occasions. His work is always accomplished and his compositions are usually more interesting than those of many of his contemporaries, often telling a 'story' by depicting a particular incident in which the vessel was involved.

Heard was born on 19 February 1800 in Egremont, just outside Whitehaven in Cumbria, the son of Joseph, a saddler, and Mabel (née Barrass), who had married on 1 December 1798 at nearby St Bees. This is substantiated by the 1851 census which gives his place of birth as Egremont, and by the fact that his youngest daughter was christened Mary Barrass Heard in 1841. He had a younger brother, Isaac (q.v.), who was also destined to become an artist.

How Heard was educated and how he spent his early years is not recorded. It has been reasonably suggested by Daniel Hay that Heard received some artistic training from John Clementson (1780–1841), a local marine painter and portraitist. Although it was previously thought that two paintings exhibited at Whitehaven in 1826 and Carlisle in 1827 were the work of the young Heard, the evidence is not clear. The newspaper reports attribute the paintings to 'I. Heard' and although 'I' was frequently used at this period instead of 'J', the fact that both paintings are portraits would seem to suggest that the artist was Joseph's brother Isaac, who throughout his career was almost exclusively referred to as a portrait painter.[1]

Heard's earliest surviving canvas, the *Countess of Lonsdale* (MMM), is inscribed and dated 'Whitehaven 1828', which suggests that he was working in the town at that date. He probably moved to Liverpool sometime in the following couple of years, because on 15

December 1832 he married Alice Wilson, a widow with a 7-year-old daughter Sarah Ann, at St Philip's, Liverpool. Both Heard and his wife are described as 'of this parish', which suggests they had been living there for at least some months, though he probably knew her from Whitehaven where Alice had married Joseph Wilson in August 1822 and where Sarah Ann was born in November 1823. Although the Heards' eldest daughter, Elizabeth, was recorded in later censuses as being born in Whitehaven, both she and her sister Mabel were baptised at St Peter's in Liverpool on 13 November 1833, when the family was living in Norfolk Street. It is likely that Heard was living and working in Liverpool from at least 1832.

The Heards had three more children, Joseph, born in January 1836, Alice, baptised in June 1838, and Mary, born in early 1841. By 1836 they had moved to Pitt Street, which was to be their home for the rest of Heard's life, though at two separate addresses.

Heard first appears in the local directories in 1834 when he is listed with his brother, Isaac, as 'artists (portrait and marine)' at 11 Norfolk Street. He is listed in a number of directories over the next twenty-five years, generally as a marine artist but occasionally also as a portrait painter.

In 1841 the family was recorded as living at 109 Pitt Street, though Sarah Ann Wilson, Heard's step-daughter, was not at home and appears to have been living in a court in New Bristol Street working as an oakum picker, a job usually undertaken only by the very poorest members of society. The circumstances of this situation can only be guessed at, but she seems to have returned to the family home after her mother died of tuberculosis aged 45 in October 1844. She was certainly living there in 1851, when she is described as 'housekeeper'. Heard's two eldest daughters were both working, Elizabeth as a dressmaker and Mabel as a pupil teacher, and his son Joseph, 15, was an apprentice. The two youngest daughters, Alice and Mary, were conventionally listed as scholars.

Heard seems to have been an active member of the community, contributing half a guinea to the Patriotic Fund for the Relief and Education and Support of Widows and Orphans of the Armed Forces in Past

Joseph Heard, *Elinor Chapman off Liverpool*, signed and dated 1845, 71 x 92 cm. This is one of Heard's most attractive canvases, showing *Elinor Chapman* in two views off a detailed view of the Liverpool waterfront. (NML/MMM)

---

1   *Cumberland Pacquet and Ware's Whitehaven Advertiser*, 5 September 1826.

Wars, and being a member of the Committee for electing John Rogers in the Municipal Election.[1]

Heard died on 10 November 1859 at 60 Upper Pitt Street from cancer of the pylorus – a form of stomach cancer which at the time meant a slow and painful death. His demise was noted not only in the Liverpool papers but also by the *Carlisle Patriot*, which described him as 'marine artist, late of Whitehaven'.[2] His will was proved in January 1860, and though his effects were valued at less than £200, he was able to leave half of a property at Bank End, St Bees, plus household effects, cash, paintings and drawings to his son Joseph and Sarah Ann, and his two surviving daughters shared the proceeds from the sale of four freehold properties in Toxteth Park. This suggests not only that his career had been successful artistically but that he had been reasonably successful financially. Certainly in 1861 his son Joseph, who was then 25 and a commercial traveller/clerk, was able to afford to support a nurse to look after his infant daughter and to employ another general servant.

Heard was a prolific painter and there are nearly two hundred known or attributed works, with over forty in public collections in the UK and good examples in many of the major American museums. He was very familiar with the various rigs of sailing ships and his portrayals are direct and accurate. His seas can be slightly stylised and often tend towards a blue-grey. He makes good use of flag codes, name pennants and house flags, and the majority of his paintings can be identified as specific vessels. Whilst many of his canvases depict a fairly traditional portrait of a vessel at sea or off a familiar and often detailed location, he often chose to show some additional activity, such as the ship in more than one position, weathering a storm, or taking on a pilot. He seems to have discussed many of his commissions with his patrons in order to depict a specific incident in which the vessel had been involved. His *Windsor Towing Siam* (MMM) recorded an occasion when the sailing ship organised a tow from a paddle steamer in order to overcome an incoming wind which had kept the vessel in harbour.[3] He occasionally persuaded the client to commission two paintings in order to tell a story in more depth, such as *Sir Henry Pottinger in a Cyclone* and *Sir Henry Pottinger under Jury Rig* (MMM). The first painting records the vessel battling against a severe storm in January 1848 when it was badly damaged; the second shows her returning under a temporary rig against a tranquil sea and a setting sun.[4]

Heard usually signed his paintings but with no set pattern, using 'J. Heard' or 'Josh Heard', often with a date.

Lit.: Hay 1979; Davidson 1986: 52–57; Davidson 1995: 18–20; Finamore 1995: 47, 54; Tibbles 1999: 93–110; Wright et al. 2006: 407.

---

1 *Liverpool Mail*, 16 December 1854; *Liverpool Mercury*, 29 November 1858.
2 *Carlisle Patriot*, 28 November 1859.

3 Tibbles 1999: 109–10.
4 Tibbles 1999: 107–08.

Joseph Heard, *P S Windsor Towing Siam*, signed, inscribed and dated 1855, 71 x 102 cm. This is one of Heard's 'story' paintings showing an actual incident when *Siam* was provided with a tow to get underway against heavy winds off the Owers Lightship in the English Channel. (ARTUK/NML/MMM)

Joseph Heard, *Five Brocklebank Vessels off Whitehaven*, 76 x 110 cm. This unusually large and impressive painting was almost certainly commissioned to mark the career of Captain Joseph Pinder (1797–1851), latterly Brocklebank's Marine Superintendent, who served on all the vessels depicted. (ARTUK/NML/MMM)

Harry Hoodless (1913–1997)

Harry Taylor Hoodless was a professional artist who taught at the Laird School of Art in Birkenhead and produced distinctive maritime-related paintings.

Hoodless was born in Leeds on 29 June 1913 to William, a plumber, and his wife Emma. In 1921 they were living at 38 Hovingham Grove. He began studying at the Leeds School of Art in 1929 and was awarded a Senior Art Scholarship at the Royal College of Art in London from 1933 to 1936. He then began teaching at Norwich School of Art, and in 1939 joined the Laird School of Art. He married Hilda L. Grimes in Norwich that same summer. They initially lived at 17 Iris Avenue, Birkenhead, and later moved to Grafton Drive, Upton.

Hoodless served in the Royal Navy from 1941 until 1945 and returned to teaching at the Laird, where he remained, retiring as principal in 1976. He was chairman of the Wirral Society of Arts and president of the Deeside Art Group. He exhibited at the RA and other local exhibitions. A major retrospective exhibition was held at the Williamson Art Gallery in 1993. He died on 16 April 1997, aged 83.

The majority of Hoodless's paintings are of ships and small boats set against dock and quayside views. Although many of his paintings are of local Mersey scenes, his settings also include a wide variety of locations throughout Britain, such as Whitby, Amlwch, Lowestoft, on the Thames and on the Solway. He generally worked in egg tempera and had a very distinctive style, with bold use of colour and shapes and clear, crisp skies. His quaysides are working areas, with capstans and bollards, and are often littered with fishing gear or abandoned equipment. He also produced some still life paintings. There are good examples of his work in MMM, WmAG, Victoria Art Gallery, Liverpool, and WAG.

Lit.: Davies 1992: 140–41; Oliver 1993; Tibbles 1999: 116.

Harry Hoodless, *Waiting the Tide*, signed and dated 1954, 68 x 97 cm. This is a typical composition with an extensive and detailed foreground featuring dock furniture, and vessels in the middle distance. (NML/MMM)

Harold Hopps (1879–1963)

Harold Hopps was a talented amateur artist who mainly painted local scenes around Wallasey as well as views of the Mersey and shipping associated with the river.

Hopps was born in Birkenhead on 26 May 1879, the eldest son of Arthur Dennis Hopps, an oil merchant, and his wife Ada. The family was living in Longlands Road, Liscard, in 1881 and Hopps continued to live there for the rest of his life. He went to Wallasey Grammar School but had an interest in local history from an early age. He was working in the family oil business as a mercantile clerk in 1901, a position he still held in 1911. The firm had been established by his grandfather, Alfred Hopps, who had moved from his native Leeds in the late 1850s. After Alfred's retirement, Harold's father and his uncle, Edmund Chantrell Hopps, were the principal partners in the firm, though Harold's own position is unclear and in 1921 he was listed as 'out of work'. By 1939 only he and his sister Helen were living in the family home, and he is described as 'a retired oil merchant'. He died in St Catherine's Hospital, Birkenhead, on 24 January 1963. Probate on his estate, which was valued at £15,000, was granted to his youngest brother John.

An obituary in the *Liverpool Echo* on the day of his death described Hopps as an 'enthusiastic painter [who] put down on canvas the changing face of Wallasey during his life-time'. Whilst the majority of his work consists of views of his local area, there are a significant number of views of shipping on the Mersey, particularly ferry boats. His earliest maritime canvas dates from 1895. He occasionally painted copies of earlier artists' work, including Samuel Walters' *Steam Paddle Ferries off New Brighton* (MMM). His work is competent and captures some of the atmosphere of the Mersey in its heyday.

The Wallasey Libraries Committee bought 80 paintings from him in 1960 and there are now nearly 140 works by him in WmAG.

Lit.: Wright et al. 2006: 441.

Harold Hopps, *P S La Marguerite*, signed and dated 1925, 37 x 50 cm. This conventional ship portrait is typical of Hopps's marine works. (WmAG)

LA MARGUERITE
1925

H. HOPPS

John Hughes (1805–after 1883)

John Hughes was one of the few painters of his generation who was born in Liverpool. He was a self-taught artist who established a good reputation as a ship portraitist in his own lifetime and found particular favour with American clients. He was unable to sustain himself from art alone and had a second occupation as a house painter.

Hughes was the eldest son of Henry Hughes, a pilot, and his wife Catherine, and was born on 23 November 1805 and baptised at St Thomas's Church on 26 January 1806. He married Margaret Ball Paterson at St David's, Liverpool, on 30 April 1835. The notice of the banns gives them as both living in Pitt Street and his occupation is given as 'marine painter'. From 1836 he appears regularly in local directories, described as an artist or painter. By 1841 Hughes and his wife had begun a family and were living in Bedford Street, Toxteth Park. Two daughters, Sophia Dunlop (born 1838) and Hannah Catherine (born 1841), are listed, but the eldest daughter, Henrietta, born in 1837, is not; perhaps this is an error or she was staying temporarily elsewhere.

The family had moved to Prospect Hill, Higher Tranmere, on the outskirts of Birkenhead by 1851, and the children were given as Henrietta, aged 14, Sophia D, aged 12, Henry, aged 5, and John, aged 1. Hannah seems to have died, as had a son Ellis, born in 1843. Interestingly, Hughes is described as an artist, and this is qualified by 'portraits of ships', making quite clear his speciality. They were still there in 1861 but had moved to 183 Church Road by 1871, and ten years later they were at 17 Harland Road. Gradually all the children left home except for Henry, who was still living with his parents aged 33 in 1881. Hughes was still alive when his wife died in March 1883, but the date of his own death has not been established.[1]

Despite listing his occupation as artist or painter on all official occasions, it seems that, like many of his contemporaries, Hughes was unable to sustain himself and his family from his artistic abilities alone. In 1839 he seems to have been part of Hughes & Pritchard, house painters, which was listed next door to his home in Bedford Street. That house painting was almost certainly his other occupation is borne out by a local directory entry in 1861 which lists him as an artist as having a 'studio' at 34 Formby Street in Liverpool, but the same premises also served as the office of Croston & Hughes, painters. Indeed, in the 1871 census he is listed as 'artist and painter', perhaps denoting his dual occupations, but even more intriguingly both his wife and son Henry are also listed as 'artist'. Whether this should be taken at face value is unclear – if he had been a more prolific artist he might perhaps have needed occasional support in his work, but this seems unlikely. Whatever the situation, Henry appears to have followed his father in his other career, as he is listed as 'Foreman painter' in the 1881 census.

The accuracy of Hughes's portraiture also gives rise to speculation about whether he had personal knowledge of life on board ship. Nothing is known of his life until he married aged 30. He might have spent time with his pilot father, which could have brought him into contact with a wide variety of different vessels. Whilst he probably trained as a house painter, it must also be possible that he spent some years at sea. Additional advice would always have been close at hand – many of his neighbours in Pitt Street and Toxteth were seafarers, and later his two daughters married brothers, William and James Bairnson, who were both mariners.

Hughes does not appear to have had any training as an artist, and indeed an article about his painting of the Black Star liner *Guy Mannering* specifically comments that he was 'self-taught as a painter'.[2] Nonetheless the writer describes him as 'high on the list of artists in his line'. The article goes on to state that the painting was on view at the shop of Mr Jeffreys, a carver and gilder in Bold Street, and that the artist was about to paint a second portrait of the same vessel and a portrait of the *Anglo America*. He exhibited two paintings at the Liverpool Academy in 1851, one of a Liverpool pilot boat and the other, a landscape of quarries in North Wales.

---

1   A John Hughes of the same age died in Birkenhead in March 1883, but he was a brewer and lived at a different address.

2   *Liverpool Mercury*, 8 June 1849.

John Hughes, *Pilot Cutter No.11*, 48 x 67 cm. A pilot cutter is shown in two views about to put a pilot on board a packet ship, and is a good example of Hughes's abilities. (NML/MMM)

Although some of Hughes's unsigned paintings have on occasions been attributed to Samuel Walters or Joseph Heard, they can usually be distinguished on stylistic grounds. His early paintings, perhaps understandably, lack a certain refinement and in general he uses a cooler palette of creams and bluey-greens. His paintings possess a distinctly clear and crisp atmospheric appearance. He was particularly popular with American clients and the vast majority of his known paintings are now in the United States. The only painting in a public collection in the UK is a portrait of a pilot cutter (MMM).

Lit.: Davidson 1986: 76–79, 88; Davidson 1995: 21; Finamore 1995: 55, 57, 65, 71, 74; Morris and Roberts 1998: 334; Tibbles 1999: 116–17; Wright et al. 2006: 450.

Stanley J. Hugill (1906–1992)

Stan Hugill was a seafarer and instructor at the Outward Bound Sea School, but is best known as a performer and historian of sea shanties. In retirement he took up painting and produced some 250 oils, principally of sailing ships.

Stanley James Hugill was born on 19 November 1906 in Hoylake, Cheshire, the son of Henry James and Florence Mary Hugill (née Southwood). In 1911 they were living at 5 Coast Guard Station, Blundellsands, north of Liverpool. By 1921 they were living at 9 Garfield Road, Bootle. His father was working for HM Customs as a watcher and Stan was 'awaiting vacancy as boy messenger in HM Customs'. However, in 1922 Hugill went to sea, serving as shantyman on *Garthpool*, the last British commercial sailing ship. He remained at sea and was captured when SS *Automedon* was sunk by a German raider off Sumatra on 11 November 1940. He was held as a prisoner of war at Marlag und Milag Nord, in North Germany, the main concentration camp for British merchant seamen, for four and a half years. After his release he decided to leave the sea. He studied at the School of African and Oriental Studies at the University of London and received a diploma in Japanese in 1948. He became an instructor at the Outward Bound Sea School at Aberdovey in 1950 and remained there until his retirement in 1975.

Hugill was widely travelled as a result of his seafaring career, and was not only fluent in Japanese and Spanish but spoke several oriental languages. His great enthusiasm was recording and singing shanties, which had been a major feature of life on board sailing ships. He wrote several books about shanties as well as *Sailortown* (1967), a lively account of life amongst the seafaring community in ports across the world.

He married Bronwen Irene Benbow in the spring of 1953 and they had two sons, Philip, born 1954, and Martin, born 1956. He died in Aberystwyth on 13 May 1992.

Hugill took up painting when he retired in 1975 and was a prolific amateur artist. He mainly painted sailing ships, both those he had known but also historical vessels. They are frequently depicted in challenging conditions, battling against heavy seas and storms. His only known work in a public collection is *Garthpool* (MMM).

Lit.: www.bbc.co.uk/liverpool/content/articles/2008/07/01/liverpool_tall_ships.shtml.

Stanley Hugill, *Garthpool*, signed, inscribed and dated 1930, 61 x 61 cm. This painting was presented to E. Louis, the cook on board *Garthpool*, after the ship was wrecked off the Cape Verde Islands in 1929. (NML/MMM)

Francis Hustwick (c. 1797–1865)

Francis Hustwick was only identified as a member of the Liverpool School of marine painters in the late 1990s, but his work ranks highly with that of his contemporaries and he has emerged as an important practitioner of the art of ship portraiture. The identification of a group of 50 paintings and the unmasking of his identity is comparable to a detective story and has been fully told elsewhere.[1]

The trail that finally led to the identification of Hustwick dates back to the early 1990s and began with the casual observation that the unsigned painting of *The Ship James T Foorde and the Barque Miracle*, completed in the 1840s, included a version of the red ensign which was then almost half a century out of date. Although originally a naval flag, the red ensign had been used increasingly by merchant vessels during the eighteenth century and with official sanction from 1823. It incorporates the Union Jack, the British national flag, in the upper quarter next to the hoist. The Union Jack was created in 1707, when England and Scotland were united, by merging their two national flags. It was then adapted in 1801 by the addition of a red diagonal cross to represent the union with Ireland.

Over the next few years a small number of Liverpool-related paintings with the pre-1801 ensign were noted. It was also observed that all these paintings had a number of other characteristics in common, some stylistic and some more practical, including the propensity to misspell ship names and inaccuracies in rendering flag codes. All the paintings were unsigned and researchers were led to the conclusion that there was an artist working in Liverpool who used the pre-1801 ensign as a substitute signature or rebus. On the basis of his two principal characteristics, the acronym OEBS (Old Ensign Bad Speller) was adopted. There were strong stylistic similarities with the work of Joseph Heard, and one initial thought was that the painter was an associate of Heard, perhaps his brother Isaac (q.v.).

The search for further work by the artist had raised the possibility that there might be paintings of American ships. Although flying the Stars and Stripes rather than the indicative ensign, a painting of the US ship *Castine* seemed to exhibit the well-known stylistic characteristics. The breakthrough came with examination of a painting of the American packet ship *Ne Plus Ultra* which had Liverpool connections. During cleaning, the characteristic style of OEBS emerged, and in particular similarities with *Castine* became clear. However, the crucial clue came when the inscription 'Ship Ne Plus Ultra Capt[n] Taft 1864 / Pixt F Hustwick Liverpool' was revealed along the lower edge of the canvas. Further confirmation followed with the re-examination of two paintings in American collections (*Baltic* at MM and *Liverpool Harbour* at PEM). They both included vessels showing the red ensign and both were signed, but had not been previously noticed, as Hustwick.

Francis Hustwick was born in Hull in about 1797, assuming that his death certificate gives his correct age, as no details of his birth have been found. His father, Robert, was a coachmaker and he and his younger brothers entered the coach-building business. Judging by comments in the local press, this was a thriving and successful undertaking, though not without occasional controversy. In 1834 the *Hull Packet* carried a report about 'Hustwick the Tory coachbuilder' who was accused of threatening to dismiss his men unless they voted as he instructed in the local election. The same week the men were also reported as going on strike for higher wages, 'to the surprise and vexation of their despotic employer'. In the same issue of 12 December the story was denied by one of the sons.

Hustwick's uncle, also Francis (1768–c. 1838/39), was a coach and heraldic painter but also advertised himself as a `house, sign, ship and furniture painter'. Thus, there might have been some encouragement for the artistic talents of the younger Francis within the family businesses.

Hustwick spent his early years in Hull. He married Mary Goodwin on 23 July 1817 and they had a daughter, Elizabeth. Mary died on 4 October 1822 and was buried two days later; her death was probably the result of giving birth to another daughter, Mary, who was buried on 13 October. Hustwick remarried on 14 December 1826, taking as his wife Ann Chapman,

---

1   Davidson and Tibbles 1999.

and they had three children, Charles born about 1829, Emma in 1833/34 and Ann in 1835/36.

Hustwick was probably working in the family coach-building business when his first wife died in 1822, and he was described as a 'coach painter'. Although there are references in the local Hull directories to a Francis Hustwick 'portrait and scene painter' at 117 High Street from 1818 to 1839, these could refer to his uncle of the same name. It also seems more probable that the Francis Hustwick listed as a freeman able to vote in elections at various dates between 1818 and 1836 was his uncle. Freemen were required to own freehold property worth 40 shillings in order to qualify, and the elder Hustwick is much more likely to have done so.

It is unclear whether Hustwick made a living as a full-time artist when in Hull. He might have been producing paintings as a hobby or sideline, perhaps in an attempt to build up sufficient work as an artist, but no canvases from this period have been attributed to him. However, he seems to have arrived in Liverpool as a fully fledged ship portraitist, which suggests that he had some previous experience. Although the exact date of this move is not known, it almost certainly took place in the early 1840s. Two paintings of *The Return of SS Great Britain to Liverpool* which took place on 15 September 1845 are attributed to him, as are a number of other paintings from around this period. The reasons for his move to Liverpool are unclear. A number of properties, including 'a large and respectable family' residence built by his father (who had died in 1835), were put up for sale in April 1844, possibly on the death of his mother, and it may be that he received some of the proceeds, which allowed him to set himself up in his chosen career. He might have been attracted to Liverpool because of its large, and growing, shipping business and the far greater opportunities for commissions that were likely to be on offer there.

Hustwick's time in Liverpool does not seem to have been particularly happy. His wife, Ann, died at 116 Saint James Street on 28 February 1848 from consumption. As informant of her death, his occupation is given as 'painter'. In the 1851 census his occupation is given as 'artist' and he is listed as a boarder at the Angel Inn in Howden, perhaps travelling between Liverpool and his native Hull. His two daughters, who were both dressmakers, were living in Liverpool as lodgers with a cooper, John Parr, and his family in Sparling Street. By 1861 Hustwick and his two daughters, who were unmarried, were living in Titchfield Street, and Hustwick described himself as a 'portrait and marine painter'.

Tragedy overtook the family in 1865. In the late spring Emma, his eldest daughter, contracted typhoid and died at home on 12 May. His other daughter Ann was admitted to the Smithdown Road Workhouse with fever on 29 May, the only option for those who could not afford to pay to go to hospital. Hustwick himself succumbed to typhoid on 26 June 1865 in the same workhouse, having been admitted with fever three days earlier. Within two months his son Charles had also died of fever in the Union Workhouse in Everton. By the end of 1865 only Ann survived.

The *Liverpool Mail* described Hustwick as a 'marine painter' when his daughter Emma died.[1] He does not appear in any of the local directories except for a single entry in 1865, when he is listed as a painter at 13 Henderson Street, Toxteth Park.

In the region of eighty paintings have now been attributed to him. Whilst the rebus of the old ensign is the most obvious identifying feature, it is not infallible. For instance, two paintings by Samuel Walters include an old ensign, and it makes a further appearance in a group of four paintings dating from after 1870 which are stylistically homogeneous. It is the combination of the old ensign rebus with the artist's stylistic characteristics that should be used to suggest attribution to Hustwick.

In general, Hustwick has a limited repertoire and the compositions are formulaic. Four main backgrounds predominate – Anglesey with Holyhead/South Stack and/or the Skerries; Anglesey with Parys Mountain and Point Lynas; New Brighton with the Perch Rock fort and lighthouse; and the Liverpool waterfront. Generally, the sea has wavetops running towards the ship, with an area of white spray outlining the cutwater

---

1   *Liverpool Mail*, 20 May 1865.

at the bow. There is usually a light-coloured wake at the stern contrasting with the darker foreground. The sky features banks of cumulus clouds often tinged with pink, lilac and gold.

Until recently the attribution of paintings of American vessels has been made on the basis of Hustwick's general idiosyncrasies. However, the careful observation of Andrew Davidson has now established that Hustwick also renders the Stars and Stripes inaccurately in his paintings. The original version of the American national flag was adopted in 1777 and comprised 13 red and white stripes with 13 white stars in a blue canton. It was subsequently altered in 1795 and 1818 to take account of the addition of new states. One of the key changes was in the number and position of the stripes, and in this context the colour of the first stripe below the canton is crucial. Between 1797 and 1818 this stripe was red, but from 1818 it was white, as it had also been before 1795. Analysing 13 paintings, Davidson has shown that Hustwick almost universally depicts the flag with a red stripe. The adoption of this pre-1818 arrangement is unlikely to be an unintentional mistake and the conclusion must be that Hustwick deliberately chose to do this. He thus had a rebus with which to sign paintings for both the British and American markets.

If there had previously been any doubt that the use of the old ensign was intentional, this further example of a related but distinct inaccuracy in the rendition of the American flag must dispel any such thought. However, the most intriguing aspect is why did Hustwick do it?

Was he just cocking a snook at his customers by making such a fundamental error and daring them to spot it? And why did he not sign his paintings? Although most artists failed to sign some of their work, none did so as consistently as Hustwick. Indeed, only four signed examples are currently known, all of American ships. The suggestion that Hustwick was working in the studio of another painter and did not want his employer to know that he was working on his own account is not really credible given the extent of his output. The answers will probably never be known. However, his reticence has ensured that he has maintained anonymity as an artist for nearly a century and a half and has kept many people guessing about the authorship of his paintings.

There are examples of his work in MMM, NMM, New Brunswick Museum, Canada, PEM and Maine Maritime Museum.

His son, Charles Thomas Hustwick (c. 1829–65), was also a part-time artist, though the only evidence is a couple of references in the local directories, when he is listed as a portrait painter, and there is no suggestion that he undertook any marine work. His main employment was as a house painter. The 1861 census gives his occupation as 'painter employing one man', and his death certificate describes him as a painter journeyman, meaning he had served an apprenticeship. No paintings by him have been identified.

Lit.: Davidson and Tibbles 1999; Finamore 1995: 52; Tibbles 1999: 110–15; Wright et al. 2006: 455.

Old ensign rebus, detail from Joseph Heard, *Bosphorus*. This version of the red ensign went out of use in 1801, following the union of Great Britain and Ireland. (ARTUK/NML/MMM)

Francis Hustwick, *Bosphorus*, 61 x 92 cm. As well as featuring the characteristic pre-1801 red ensign, the artist misspells the vessel's name on the pennant but spells it correctly on the hull! (ARTUK/ NML/MMM)

John R. Isaac (1809–1870)

John Raphael Isaac was a lithographer, printer and publisher who was also a framer, art dealer and heraldic painter. He was an accomplished artist and produced a number of ship portraits and other marine-inspired work, which he sold as lithographs.

Isaac was born in Liverpool in 1809, the eldest son of Ralph Isaac, a silversmith and watchmaker, and his wife Sophia. He first appears in the local directories as an engraver and printer in 1828, when he was based at his father's premises in George's Crescent North. He married Sarah Amelia, daughter of silversmith Sylvester Coleman, at the Seel Street Synagogue on 22 May 1839, and in 1841 they were living in Barnaby Street, with their son Raffaelle, aged 1. He had his own premises at 37 Castle Street by the late 1830s and transferred to number 62 in the early 1840s, remaining there until 1868. He lived at a number of addresses in the town – he was at 12 Cambridge Street in 1843, then in the late 1840s and early 1850s at 113 Chatham Street, and from the late 1850s until his death at 27 Bedford Street North.

The 1851 census lists his occupation as 'draughtsman, engraver, lithographer and printer, employing 9 men'. He and Sarah had a large household – seven children, aged from a few months to 11 years old, Sarah's sister and an aunt, and a cook and general servant. By 1861 the family had grown by one more child, Sarah's mother and two other relatives were living with them, and they had a visitor staying and two servants. In the description of his occupation Isaac includes 'painter' alongside 'publisher etc.', and at this time he was employing four men.

Although Isaac mainly worked as a lithographer and publisher, producing reproductions of other artists' works, including those of Samuel Walters, he also acted as an art dealer and entrepreneur. He advertised his services regularly in the local press, informing the public about work he had completed, limited editions, such as the latest railway map, fashionable paintings on view and the Art Union.[1] In 1846 he was appointed 'medal-list, lithographer and engraver at Liverpool' to Prince Albert and designed the menu for the reception held at the Town Hall following the opening of the Albert Dock.[2]

It seems that Isaac could also turn his hand to other things, and in 1855 he had a meeting with Major-General Sir Frederick Smith of the Board of Ordnance to explain his design for portable huts to be used by the army.[3] In 1868 he placed a series of advertisements in the local press for 'indexed key cabinets, portable or fixed – John R Isaac, Patentee'.[4] In the mid-1860s he was also acting as an agent for Havana cigars and tobacco.[5]

Isaac served as the honorary secretary of the Liverpool branch of the Art Union from the mid-1840s until just before he died, and in later years this came to dominate his activities. Indeed, in 1860 he gave up the engraving and lithographic element of his business 'to concentrate his whole attention on the higher branches of the fine arts generally'. His employees, led by the manager, George Trowbridge, presented him with 'a very elegant solid silver fish knife and fork' as a mark of their esteem.[6] He continued to advertise Art Union events in the local press throughout the following decade, but in November 1868 he announced that he was moving to 'premises of a more limited extent' due to redevelopment in Castle Street.[7] His eldest son, Raffaelle, seems to have taken a larger interest in the business about this time, when it is referred to as 'John R Isaac & Son'.[8]

Isaac died at Raffaelle's home in Upper Parliament Street on 9 April 1870, the very day when an advertisement appeared offering for sale furniture from his Bedford Street house, as Mr Isaac 'is obliged to leave Liverpool on account of ill-health'.[9] He was interred

---

1   For example, *Gore's Liverpool General Advertiser*, 3 January 1839; *Liverpool Mail*, 30 December 1841; *Liverpool Mercury*, 20 June 1845

2   *Liverpool Mercury*, 21 August 1846.
3   *Morning Chronicle*, 11 June 1855.
4   *Liverpool Mercury*, 2 September 1868.
5   *Liverpool Daily Post*, 27 December 1864.
6   *Liverpool Daily Post*, 6 June 1860.
7   *Liverpool Mercury*, 13 November 1868.
8   *Liverpool Mercury*, 18 January 1869.
9   *Liverpool Daily Post*, 11 April 1870; *Liverpool Daily Post*, 9 April 1870.

in the Jewish burial ground in Dean Road Cemetery, Kensington, Liverpool.

Raffaelle kept the Liverpool business going until at least 1873, but the 1881 census shows that he had moved to London where he was working as a dealer in works of art. Unlike his father, he does not seem to have been very successful, and when he died in 1904 he left just £19.

Although John Isaac made limited use of his artistic skills, he was clearly an accomplished artist and draughtsman. He produced a number of prints based on his own art work, including portraits of the captured slave ship *Ashburton*, the emigrant ship *Lightning* and the clipper *Red Jacket* caught in ice. Perhaps his most ambitious work was a series of eight plates which he published of the *Niagara* laying the Atlantic telegraph cable off the south-west coast of Ireland in 1857. They were produced from 'a series of sketches drawn on the spot by John R Isaac and printed by him'. The plates are accompanied by a detailed description of the operation, written by Isaac. The following year he produced an aerial view of Liverpool and followed this with a companion view of Manchester in 1860.[1] Several of his lithographs and two of his drawings, including that of the *Ashburton*, are in LCL.

Lit.: Davidson 1986: 131–32; Rubinstein et al. 2011: 451; http://atlantic-cable.com/Books/1857Isaac/index.htm.

---

1   *Liverpool Mail*, 8 May 1858; *Manchester Courier and Lancashire General Advertiser*, 5 May 1806.

William Jackson (1745–1803)

William Jackson was one of the first generation of ship portrait painters to work in Liverpool. He was also employed as a painter of ship portraits on ceramics and he probably worked occasionally as a miniaturist.

The established facts of Jackson's life and career are few. He was probably born in Liverpool in 1745, and on 1 December 1771 he married Ellen Stanton at St Peter's, Liverpool, when he gave his occupation as 'painter'. He is next mentioned in 1774 when he exhibited at the Liverpool Society of Artists. He is listed as `William Jackson, 67 Frog Lane now styled Whitechapel, ship portraits', clearly indicating his main interest. His exhibits comprised a portrait of a lady, a miniature of a gentleman and three landscapes, entitled *Moonlight: a Study from Nature*, *Small Breeze* and *Close by the Wind: a Hard Gale*, all of which could be interpreted as maritime subjects. By 1777 he was living at 41 Whitechapel and was described as 'Portrait and Sea-piece painter'. In 1781 he was residing at 8 Williamson Street, and from there he entered two 'sea pieces' in the first exhibition of the Society for Promoting Painting and Design. The catalogue lists 'Lightning' brig, and her prize, sea piece William Jackson, Liverpool and 'Tartar' sloop, sea piece William Jackson, Liverpool. At the second exhibition in 1787 he submitted only one work, a *View from the River Mersey on the Cheshire side with a distant Prospect of Liverpool*.

By 1790 he was at 35 Sir Thomas Buildings, listed as a 'Prospect Painter', and was described as a 'limner' in the 1794 directory. Finally, he is included in the directories from 1796 to 1803 as a 'perspective painter' at 21 and then 13 Gibraltar Street. The 1801 census gives no occupation for him but informs us that he was living in Gibraltar Row, in a household of two males and four females – him and his wife and perhaps a son and three daughters. He died in 1803 and was buried at St Peter's on 13 August 1803, when he was again described as a 'limner' of Gibraltar Street.

The variety of terminology used to describe his employment is not unusual at this period, but might perhaps recognise Jackson's flexibility. The term 'limner', used generically to describe a painter, normally also indicates a speciality in portraits and miniatures. Whilst Jackson's preference might have been for ship portraiture, he might have found that the human variety was a valuable supplement to his income, and the 1774 exhibits and Bernard Watney's suggestion that he painted portraits on jugs might bear this out.

Two signed works by Jackson are known – *The Barque Boyne* in Whitehaven Museum, dated 1794, and

The Liverpool Slave Ship (MMM). A small number of other paintings have been attributed to Jackson on stylistic grounds, but no further signed works have been forthcoming. The most impressive is the portrait of the ship *Watt*, a confident and masterly canvas completed in the last years of his life. Unusually it shows the ship in three positions rather than the more usual one or two views, as do two other works attributed to him. The *Brig in Three Positions* and the *Merchantman in Three Positions* are almost identical to one another in composition, even down to such details as the punt being towed from the stern. Although only shown in two views, the *British Brig* in MM is extremely similar.

However, it is in the very stylised and characteristic way in which Jackson painted sails that the principal grounds for attribution lie. Most commonly, as in the *Liverpool Slave Ship*, the main courses are partly furled but in a very distinctive way. On the main mast the main course is almost scalloped with sagging folds, and on the foremast the main is shown with ball-like shapes pushed forward and filled with wind. The mizzen is without a main course. By contrast the topsails are smooth and full, frequently adopting a scroll-like profile with deep shadows on the lower edges. The royals are usually caught filled with wind in a long narrow bolster shape. Where main courses are shown, they generally follow the smoother pattern of the topsails, but the main course is often triced up as in the *Watt* (MMM).

Jackson usually shows considerable activity on deck in the principal view, with authentic and carefully thought-out detail. For instance, the master of the *Watt* is shown with a speaking trumpet, the master of the *Liverpool Slave Ship* is clearly visible in his tricorn hat with some of his other officers on the poop, men are often shown in the rigging or on the bowsprit and, interestingly, the *Naval Frigate* (NMM) has about twenty Africans on deck.

Bernard Watney noted similar characteristics, particularly the treatment of the sails, on a number of ceramic bowls produced in Liverpool in the second half of the eighteenth century. At this period, Liverpool was a major centre for the production of ceramics, including creamware, delftware and enamelled porcelain. There was both a thriving home market and an important export market, principally to America. Watney has convincingly suggested that Jackson was responsible for the painting on a group of important bowls, jugs and mugs, produced at a number of different factories between 1770 and 1790. These include two important enamelled painted ship bowls featuring the brig *Swallow* and HMS *Hyena*. The *Swallow* bowl in particular exhibits all the sail characteristics noted above. Watney's suggestion that Jackson might have been responsible for a group of delftware bowls dating from the previous two decades, the earliest example being *Success to the Eagle, 1754*, is not sustainable given that the burial register gives his age at 58 in 1803.

Jackson was clearly producing ship portraits on canvas from the time of the 1774 exhibition, though the earliest surviving paintings seem to date from about 1780. This is the date suggested for the *Slave Ship*, and the *Mentor* painting is likely to have been completed shortly after October 1778 when she captured *Carnatic*. (*Mentor* was herself lost on her next voyage in 1779.) On the basis of the dating of the ship bowls, it is likely that the artist began his career as a decorator of ceramics before extending his range to work on canvas. There is clearly scope to explore further the artistic activities of this talented but little-known artist.

Lit.: Davidson 1986: 19–21; Watney 1993; Morris and Roberts 1998: 348; Tibbles 1999: 118–20; Wright et al. 2006: 462.

William Jackson, *Watt*, signed, 91 x 117 cm. This impressive painting originally belonged to Wilfred Kilpatrick, master of the vessel between 1802 and 1805. (NML/MMM)

H. F. James (1772/73–1823)

Henry Freeman James is known as the original painter of a coloured aquatint entitled *View of Liverpool* and probably an associated oil painting which might be the original for the engraving.

James was born in 1772/73 and probably came from near Stourbridge in the West Midlands.[1] The earliest reference to him dates from 2 January 1793 when he married Elizabeth Gould at St Martin's Church, Birmingham. Whilst she is 'of this parish', he is described as an artist 'of the parish of Old Swinford' in Worcestershire. Their son Henry Gould James was baptised in the adjacent parish of Pedmore, Worcestershire, on 9 December 1798.

James is listed in *Gore's Directories* as living at Low Hill from 1803 until 1814, initially as 'draughtsman, surveyor and teacher of the French language'. From 1811 he appears as a 'draughtsman and picture broker', with an 'auction, commission and picture room' in Lord Street. It was here that Sarah Baartman, the so-called 'Hottentot Venus', was 'exhibited' in 1812, which suggests that James was flexible in what he regarded as suitable for display.[2] He moved to Manchester, probably in early 1815, establishing one of the first lithographic businesses in the town and becoming a prominent freemason, being admitted to the Lodge of Integrity in Manchester on 5 September 1815. He died there on 26 July 1823, and his son took over the business until his own death in 1842.

The number and variety of James's occupations suggests a precariousness in his career, and we know that around the time of his move to Manchester he had a number of debts. The chance survival of an undated letter to one of his creditors blames a court case in Lancaster for his financial position, but goes on to say that he hopes to be able to discharge his debts from the proceeds from his *View of Liverpool*, 'as I have a good subscription to it'.[3] Unfortunately, this proved not to be the case, and in early 1816 he found himself in court for bankruptcy.[4] His prospects did not improve materially and James died in debt, his debts being later paid off by his son.

In 1811 James exhibited *View of Liverpool, taken from Seacombe Common – From which it is intended to publish an engraving by subscription* (MMM) at the Liverpool Academy. An aquatint, with a few minor differences, was engraved shortly afterwards by William J. Bennett (1787–1844), a London-based artist and engraver who later had a successful career in the United States. A handbill for the engraving informs us that 'H. F. James, Professor of Arts' was 'assisted in the shipping department by that ingenious artist Mr Anderson, of London'. William Anderson (1757–1837) was a well-known marine artist, and one suspects that his assistance was probably little more than advice rather than involving any practical role, given that the few vessels shown are incidental to the main scene and are depicted with relative simplicity. James also produced a colour engraving *Bidston Lighthouse and Signals*, about 1807.

Lit.: Davidson 1986: 29–31; Morris and Roberts 1998: 349; Tibbles 1999: 125; Wright et al. 2006: 463.

---

1 Birth date calculated on the basis that he was 48 in September 1815 when he was admitted as a Freemason, *Register of Admissions: Country and Foreign, 1751–1921*, Library and Museum of Freemasonry, London.
2 *Liverpool Mercury*, 14 August 1812. I am grateful to Glen Huntley for drawing my attention to this information.

---

3 LCL, quoted in full Davidson 1986: 30
4 *Public Ledger and Daily Advertiser*, 28 January 1816.

H. F. James, *View of Liverpool, 1811*, 44 x 80 cm. This is James's only known marine painting, which was the original for the engraving 'A View of the Town and Harbour of Liverpool, Taken from a North West Station of Seacomb Common'. (NML/MMM)

John Jenkinson (1764–1820)

This talented artist has become better known in recent years and is now recognised as one of the leading marine painters of his generation in Liverpool. In the past his work was frequently confused with that of Robert Salmon, but the two artists have distinctive styles and the emergence of more examples of Jenkinson's work has confirmed his qualities.

John Jenkinson was probably born in 1764 and was already describing himself as a painter when he married Esther Bushell at St Paul's, Liverpool, on 3 January 1786. They had at least four children – Richard, born on 8 May 1787 when they were living in Fairhurst Street, Thomas, baptised on 14 June 1789, Jennett (Janet) Bushell, baptised on 24 April 1791 (died 4 January 1799) and Mary, baptised on 23 April 1794, when they were living in Quinn Street. On each occasion Jenkinson described his occupation as 'painter'.

There are a number of possible entries in local directories, but the inability to distinguish between house painters and artist painters leaves some measure of uncertainty in making positive identifications. There is an entry for John Jenkinson, painter, 1 New Quay, in the 1790 directory, and at Queen Anne Street in 1794 and 1796. After being absent for several years, the first definitive entry appears in 1807 when he is listed as 'ship painter' at 13 Crosshall Street, and this is repeated until 1810. In 1813 and 1814 the entry appears as John Jenkinson 'mariner portrait painter' at 25 Middle Lane, Everton. The use of mariner might be a printer's error for marine or an accepted usage, but it could indicate exactly what it says and explain the artist's absence at sea. From 1816 to 1821, the description 'marine and portrait painter' is used with an address at 18 Russell Street. In 1821 a Robert Jenkinson is listed at the same address, but he does not appear in later directories and, unless he is an undocumented relative, this is probably a misprint for Jenkinson's son Richard, who was also a painter. Mary Jenkinson of Brownlow Hill, a teacher, might have been his daughter.

Jenkinson clearly regarded himself as a serious artist and displayed works in the annual exhibitions of the Liverpool Academy between 1810 and 1814, being listed amongst the academicians in 1812. The catalogue entries confirm that he specialised in local marine and landscape subjects and portraits, as suggested by the local directories. Unfortunately, the brevity of the titles, such as *A Storm*, *Shipping View of Liverpool*, does not allow any identification to be made with extant works.

Jenkinson died a year earlier than previously thought. Parish records show that he was buried at St Paul's Church on 14 November 1820 when his age was given as 56. News of his death did not appear in the Liverpool papers, but it was carried in the *Cumberland Pacquet* for 4 December 1820: 'At a small house, Brownlow Hill, Liverpool, Mr J. Jenkinson, marine painter.' His will, dated 14 April 1819, was proved in August 1822. This shows that John Jenkinson, 'portrait painter, of Stanhope Street, Liverpool', died on 10 November 1820, and his personal property and effects, valued at less than £100, were left to his wife Esther and thereafter his daughter Mary, who was also appointed as executrix.

It is clear that Jenkinson was an accomplished and versatile artist, and enough examples of his ship paintings have now come to light to make it easier to recognise his style. Careful examination has also shown that a number are signed, though his habit of placing the signature on the stern of a boat can provide a challenge to those who are unprepared for this idiosyncrasy.

Jenkinson generally provides a substantial and accurate depiction of the vessel forming the main subject in the centre of the canvas and includes interesting and authentic details, whether of rigging or work on board. The vessel is almost always shown in the Mersey, mainly against the Liverpool waterfront, though occasionally against the Wirral shore. Although his backgrounds are topographically accurate, they are not delineated in the almost brick-by-brick fashion favoured by Salmon, but in a rather broader manner. The ship constitutes a microcosm in itself, at home in its natural element and seemingly remote from the complexities of life ashore. Jenkinson also prefers to employ a cool and pale palette, with tranquil bluey-green seas and light clear skies. This is in contrast to the warmer colours generally used by Salmon. Perhaps the other obvious distinction between the two artists is the treatment of the sea, which Jenkinson shows more naturalistically and without the regimentation favoured by Salmon.

John Jenkinson, *Armed Brig in the Mersey off Birkenhead*, signed, 81 x 112 cm. This is one of Jenkinson's finest canvases, showing an armed vessel about to depart from the Mersey, and includes the charming detail of the master doffing his hat to the departing tender. (NML/MMM)

As with the majority of such works at this period, it is rarely possible to identify any of the vessels which Jenkinson painted. Sometimes it is even difficult to distinguish between merchantmen and naval vessels. Although he often included flags on his vessels, they do not seem to conform to known codes and usage and are frequently perplexing. For instance, he includes a blue ensign with a red lower border on several occasions and even a green ensign with a similar border. This latter probably represents an Irish connection as it appears on the Irish packet leaving Liverpool, and there are other recorded examples with a similar flag but incorporating an Irish harp on the fly. However, these flags appear to be unofficial and their exact meaning is not clear.

Jenkinson was also responsible for a number of topographical views often produced as prints, principally of Liverpool and the Mersey. These include views from various places on the Wirral coast including Seacombe and the Magazines. He was able to include not only shipping and small local craft in the river but also interesting activities on shore, such as shrimpers. He also produced a view of Preston from Penwortham and a view of Maryport showing a ship awaiting her launch. The year after he died a sale of household effects in Liverpool, advertised in the *Liverpool Mercury* for 22 June 1821, shows that some of these works were on a large scale: 'View of Liverpool by Jenkinson, in gilt frame 9 feet 6 by 6 feet 7, ditto, View of Preston by Ditto, in gilt frame, 6 feet 3 by 4 feet 8.'

So far, his work as a portraitist has not been uncovered except for one canvas which passed through the salerooms in 1999. This is signed 'J. Jenkinson Liverpool' and includes a date which appears to be March 1813, though the third digit is open to some discussion as a possible 3. It shows the head and shoulders of a man, but the suggestion that this is a self-portrait is unsubstantiated.

Very few of his paintings are known and the only significant collection of his work in public collections is in MMM.

Lit.: Davidson 1986: 26–29; Davidson 1995: 16; Morris and Roberts 1998: 350; Tibbles 1999: 126–31; Wright et al. 2006: 465.

John Jenkinson, *View of Liverpool*, signed, 91 x 127 cm. This is one of several paintings of Liverpool completed by Jenkinson, and dates from about 1815. (NML/MMM)

John Josse, *S S Andorinha of the Yeoward Line, Liverpool*, signed and dated 1923, 36 x 62 cm. This fairly standard portrait is the only known work by Josse. (WmAG)

John Josse (1874–1956)

John Francis Josse was a seaman who is known for one oil painting.

Josse was born in Liverpool on 19 July 1874, the second son of Aimable Josse, a French-born seafarer, and his English wife Mary (formerly Rowson, née Ford).[1] He was baptised as a Catholic at the church of

Our Lady of Reconciliation de la Salette on 8 September the same year. He was rechristened as an Anglican at St Mathias, Liverpool, on 2 April 1879, just after his father's death, which had occurred on board ship at Buenos Aires on 3 January. The family was already in financial difficulties and his mother and the children had spent time in the Liverpool Workhouse in 1878 and 1879. Josse was admitted to Kirkdale Industrial School, which provided for the care and training of pauper children, on 29 October 1882. His mother died in 1883 and he remained at the school until he was sent to

---

1   The 1939 register gives his date of birth as 19 July 1877, but all other documents, including his military service record, give 1874.

HMS *Indefatigable*, the training ship for the orphans of seamen, on 29 May 1888. He was 'a very hard-working, quiet boy' of very good character and in August 1890 he won a prize for rowing.[1] On 18 October 1890 he joined the ship *Rialto* bound for Callao, Peru, and on a follow-up visit in 1895 his performance was described as 'very good throughout'. It seems from the same report that he had already been shipwrecked twice in that period.

In 1901 Josse was boarding at 24 Louisa Street, Everton. He married Amelia Elizabeth Crabbe, the daughter of a storekeeper, at St Philip's Church on 19 June 1904, and they went on to have seven children. In 1911 he was living at 34 Graham Street, Dingle, and working as a seaman for the local Dock Board. He enlisted in the Royal Engineers as a sapper in June 1917, but after training in Scotland he was hospitalised with

gastritis in October. He recovered but on the voyage to Mesopotamia he was diagnosed with valvular disease of the heart and was again in hospital in Basra and then Bombay, from where he was transferred to the Bermondsey Military Hospital. He was discharged on 7 May 1919 and left the army through disability. His wife and family were living at 1 Bickerton Street, off Lark Lane, in 1921, but he was absent, presumably at sea.

In 1939 Josse was living at 212 Kingsheath Avenue, Knotty Ash, with his wife and eldest son, and he is described as a 'seaman incapacitated'. He was living at 93 Withington Road, Speke, when he died aged 82 in 1956 and he was buried in West Derby Cemetery on 17 September.

Josse's only known work is a very competent painting of the Yeoward liner SS *Andorinha* (WmAG) in a profile view at sea, signed 'J F Josse 1923'. Although his eldest son shared his name and was 18 at the time, it seems most likely that the father is the artist, given his strong maritime experience.

---

1 *Liverpool Mercury*, 8 August 1890.

Emil Krause (1866–1922)

Emil Albert Krause was born in Berlin on 2 March 1861 to Franz Krause, a landscape artist, and his wife Amelie.[2] His parents and family moved to England, settling in Manchester in 1878, and were living at 28 Bignor Street in 1881.[3] They relocated to Southport in 1886 and were living at 42 Liverpool Road, Birkdale, in 1891, when Krause is listed as 'watercolour painter'. He and his father had been in partnership since 1887, but Krause senior had borrowed considerable sums of money and they were declared bankrupt in February

1889.[4] Krause's father died in 1900, and although he does not appear in the 1901 census, he is listed as living with his mother at 10 Hoghton Street, Southport, in 1911. He died in 1922.[5]

Krause specialised in landscapes, particularly of North Wales, but a few marine and coastal scenes survive, including *The Wreck of the Mexico* and *The Custom House, Liverpool* (both Atkinson Art Gallery, Southport). His elder brother was Max Sinclair (q.v.).

Lit.: Wright et al. 2006: 493.

---

2 Although generally known as Emil Albert, he was baptised Frederich August Emil.
3 *Liverpool Weekly Courier*, 16 February 1889.

4 *Liverpool Weekly Courier*, 16 February 1889.
5 www.art.org, though I have been unable to substantiate this from official records. He is not listed in the 1921 census.

James Mann (1883–1946)

James Smith Scrimgeour Mann came from a seafaring family in Dundee, but moved to Merseyside in his mid-twenties, where he practised as a professional artist for the rest of his life. He produced some atmospheric oils but also worked regularly in watercolour and produced lithographs and work for shipping companies.

Mann was born at 9 Viewforth Road, Dundee, on 30 August 1883, the son of James Smith Mann, a ship's master, and Marjory, his wife. His unusual middle name Scrimgeour was the maiden name of his maternal grandmother, Helen Peter. She lived with the family for at least the last decade of her life, and although she had at least four other children, she clearly had a special relationship with Marjory, nominating her as her next of kin and executrix.

Many of Mann's father's voyages were long-distance, including to Australia, and Marjory accompanied him on at least one of these, giving birth to a son on board the *Thomasina Maclellan* on 20 January 1889. Davidson states that the family spent some time abroad, and it seems likely that this was the case in 1891 when there is no reference to the family in the census. By 1901 they were back in Dundee, living at Blackness Road, though Captain Mann was away at sea. James Mann, who was then 17, is described as a scholar and was presumably still at the Harris Academy, where he is known to have received part of his education. In what must have been a body blow for his mother, James Mann senior died of heart disease at sea in September 1901, and less than a month later her own mother also died.

By 1911 Mann was living with his widowed mother and his elder unmarried sister, Isobel, in an eight-roomed house in Hertford Drive, Liscard. Mann gives his occupation as 'artist painter', and the move to Merseyside might have been partly prompted by the greater opportunities for an artist that Liverpool offered. It might also have been influenced by the fact that Mann's younger brother, Robert, who had followed the family seafaring tradition, was working for the locally based Bibby Line. Certainly, Mann was already finding work, and in 1911 he designed a poster for the White Star Line and its new luxury liners *Olympic* and *Titanic*, which were about to enter service.

Mann's career was put on hold by the outbreak of the First World War, and when his mother died in November 1915 he was a lance-corporal in 2/1 Regiment Scottish Horse. Davidson states that he transferred to the 5th Battalion, the Liverpool King's Regiment, and was injured, giving him a limp which he retained for the rest of his life. He had presumably been medically discharged by March 1917 when he got married and gave his occupation as 'artist'. His wife was Catherine Mary Allen Pengelly, daughter of James Pengelly, a purser. They were living with her father at 20 Gardner Road, Old Swan, where they remained until the mid-1930s when they moved to Four Winds, Thorsway, West Kirby. This large house, high on Caldy Hill, overlooked Liverpool Bay and on a clear day gave views of the North Wales coast and Anglesey.

Mann was living there with his wife in 1939, when he is described as 'marine landscape painter'. They were employing Elizabeth Taaafe, a 53-year-old single woman, as a domestic servant. The other person living there was Norwegian-born Nikoline Moller, aged 86, who is described as 'companion, retired'. It has not been possible to discover what her relationship was to them, though she had been living with them and James Pengelly in 1921. She died at Thorsway in October 1946 and probate for her £1,000 estate was granted to Catherine Mann.

James Mann exhibited marine subjects regularly in the Autumn Exhibitions at the Walker Art Gallery in the interwar years. He was a member of the Liverpool Academy and became a member of the Royal Cambrian Academy in 1932. He served as vice-president of the RCA in 1940 and became president in 1942. He was attending the opening of the Academy's summer exhibition at Plas Mawr, Conway, in June 1946 when he was taken ill and died a few hours later in Llandudno Hospital. Strangely, there is no reference to Mann in the probate records, but when his wife died in the Brookfield Nursing Home in West Kirby in November 1962, her address was given as Four Winds, Thorsway, and her estate valued at £22,293.

Mann produced a whole range of work during his career, in both oil, watercolour and lithography. He painted some fine ship portraits in oils such as *Sarpedon*

James Mann, *Sarpedon in Gladstone Dock, Liverpool*, signed, 72 x 87 cm. Mann adopts an oblique angle to add extra interest to this atmospheric portrait, which was commissioned by the vessel's owners, the Blue Funnel Line. (NML/MMM)

in Gladstone Docks for the Blue Funnel Line (MMM), the atmospheric *Tide Time* (WAG) and *MV Derbyshire*, shown converted as a troop carrier, for the Bibby Line. During the Second World War he also recorded some of the wartime activity on the Mersey, including watercolours of a convoy passing the bar lightship and other naval scenes.

Lit.: Davidson 1986: 119–20, 124.

William McDowell (1888–1950)

William John Patton McDowell trained and worked as a draughtsman and naval architect at Vickers in Barrow before moving to Merseyside in the mid-1920s, when he became a full-time commercial artist for the next fifteen years. He mainly produced paintings of historical marine subjects, but he occasionally worked for local shipping companies, and during the Second World War, when he served in the Royal Navy Scientific Service, he produced some contemporary naval subjects.

McDowell was born on 26 November 1888, the son of Henry Black McDowell and his wife Jessie, of Cavendish Street, Barrow. His father ran a successful tailoring and outfitting business which in 1881 employed six men, two boys and a shop assistant. Henry died of heart disease aged 35 in the summer of 1889, leaving his widow Jessie to run the business and bring up five children. They lived on the premises at Cavendish Street for many years, but by 1911 she was living at 65 Abbey Road with her three unmarried children and a domestic servant. McDowell, who was then 22, was working as a ship's draughtsman. Davidson was in contact with McDowell's daughter, who confirmed his early interest in drawing but also his determination to have a good career by studying naval architecture at evening classes and qualifying as an Associate Member of the Institute of Naval Architects.

McDowell married Gertrude Duerden in the summer of 1913 and they had a son and daughter. He drew and painted as a hobby, and in 1920 *Vickers News* published a coloured picture of one of the steamers the company was building for the Australian Commonwealth Line, 'by Mr William McDowell of the Barrow Works staff'.[1] The 1921 census confirms that he was working as an 'artist sketcher' for Vickers Ltd, and was living at 17 Victoria Road, Barrow. Not long afterwards McDowell gave up his job, and in about 1925 he moved to Wallasey to work as a full-time artist. He was commissioned to paint murals for *Mauretania*, *Stratheden* and *Queen of Bermuda*. McDowell was also a writer and broadcaster. He initially wrote short stories,

such as 'The Nelson Touch' for the *Windsor Magazine* (1937), and in 1939 he wrote a novel *Roughanapes*, which was awarded a special first novel prize by the publishers Hodder & Stoughton.[2] The story was based on his own experiences as a shipbuilder and artist. About this time he began radio broadcasting and gave talks on the Lancashire Nobby and Morecambe Bay Prawner and a series of talks on 'sea lore for the landsman'.[3]

McDowell and his family were living at 24 Dovedale Road, Wallasey, in September 1939, when he described himself as a 'novelist and artist'. He took a position with the Royal Naval Scientific Service during the war and in 1945 and 1946 was living in Queen's Gate Terrace, Kensington, London. He later moved to 6 Dalmeny Road, Carshalton, in Surrey, and in 1947 published *The Shape of Ships*, a history of ship development over the ages. One of his last tasks was to produce plans for a replica of Captain Cook's *Endeavour* which was exhibited in the Dome of Discovery at the 1951 Festival of Britain. He died in the Surrey County Hospital on 21 December 1950 and probate was granted to his widow, Gertrude, in the sum of £2,980.

McDowell worked in both oils and watercolour. He produced mainly historical subjects, often specific events such as *News of Nelson*, *The Arrival of Royal Yacht Mary* and *The Return of Vindictive from Zeebrugge, 1918*, or more general views of historical vessels, such as *Ships and Dolphins at Sunset*. He did some contemporary scenes such as *Ferry leaving Dover*. In addition to the commissioned murals, he produced a small number of posters, including a view of the *Queen Mary* for Cunard and a more general poster for Shaw Savill Line. During the war he produced a number of drawings of wartime activities and events for the illustrated magazine, *The Sphere*. There are representative examples of his work in the NMM, WmAG and the Dock Museum, Barrow.

He illustrated his own books as well as others with a maritime theme.

Lit.: Davidson 1986: 132.

---

1   *Lancashire Evening Post*, 10 January 1920.

2   *Burnley Express*, 28 July 1937; *Liverpool Daily Post*, 1 March 1939.
3   *The Scotsman*, 23 July 1938; *Manchester Evening News*, 13 February 1939.

William McDowell, *An Epic of the Mersey: Emile Delmar*, signed, 152 x 102 cm. This action-packed canvas celebrates a rescue mission by the New Brighton lifeboat in 1928. (WmAG)

Duncan McFarlane (c. 1818–1865)

Duncan McFarlane was a native of Scotland but lived in Liverpool for most of the last twenty years of his life. His ship portraits were particularly popular with American captains and mariners visiting the port, and most of his known works are now to be found in the United States. Given the relatively small number of his paintings that survive, it is very likely he had some other occupation, but no information has been found to indicate what this might have been.

Little is known about his origins and early life. We know from local directories, censuses and parish records relating to the birth of his children that he was resident in Liverpool from 1848 until his death in 1865. The two censuses in which he appears give his place of birth as 'Scotland' but with no further details. When he married, his father's name was given as John McFarlane and his father's occupation as 'pilot'. It is, thus, possible that McFarlane was the son of John and Mary McFarlane who was born in Glasgow on 17 December 1818.

Nothing is known of McFarlane's childhood or early career, though given his later extensive knowledge of ships and their rigging, it is possible that he spent time at sea. He is first listed in Liverpool as a 'marine painter' at 3 Bath Street in 1848, and the following year he is described as a 'portrait painter', living at 23 Hunter Street. He is similarly listed in the directories of 1851 and 1853, now living at 9 Rose Hill Terrace, but again uses the title 'marine painter' in 1855, and in 1857 and 1859, when he is located at 103 Duke Street, Everton. This might have been a studio, as parish register entries relating to the birth of his children suggest that he was still living at Rose Hill Terrace at this time. From 1860 he lived at 38 Luther Street, describing himself as either 'painter' or 'artist'.

McFarlane married Hannah Evans, the daughter of John Evans, a labourer, at St Philip's Church in Liverpool on 7 March 1848. The 1851 census confirms that they were living in Rose Hill Terrace with their 2-year-old daughter Mary Jane. Over the next decade or so, the couple had at least five more children, though only two of them survived. The family had moved to Luther Street, Everton, by the time of the next census in 1861 and included Mary Jane, now 12, David, aged 8, and Margaret, aged 3. In both censuses, McFarlane's occupation is given as 'marine painter'.

McFarlane died at home, accompanied by his wife, on 24 March 1865 aged 47. The cause of death was given as 'softening of the brain' and his occupation was stated as 'Marine Painter, Master'.

Like John Hughes, many of McFarlane's surviving works are portraits of American vessels, and his work is far better known in the United States than in his native country. The preponderance of American subjects has given rise to the suggestion that he might have spent some time in the United States. However, there is no documentary evidence to confirm a period of residence there, and suggestions that he was an artist in Boston are unsubstantiated. The vast majority of his paintings are set in the Mersey or the approaches to Liverpool, with just one painting having a Boston background and another showing the Confederate steam ship *Nashville* burning the Union clipper *Harvey Birch* three days out of Le Havre. Given his family commitments, it seems improbable that McFarlane would have left Liverpool to work in Boston after 1848. It is just possible that he might have spent time there as a young man, perhaps as a seafarer, but on balance it seems much more likely that he gained an American clientele in Liverpool through recommendation, and that his knowledge of the Boston waterfront came from engravings.

McFarlane's work is very similar to that of Samuel Walters and Joseph Heard, and several of his unsigned paintings have been attributed to one of these artists. The colour and treatment of the sea in particular bears a strong resemblance to Heard. However, Heard's seas tend to be more finely depicted and McFarlane often portrays a more rippling type of sea. His mature paintings display excellent draughtsmanship, giving the sails and rigging a crisp, clean look. The wind tends to fill the canvas more fully than in the work of many of his contemporaries. When a ship's name is included on the stem or stern, it is carefully delineated, and he also makes frequent use of the Marryat Code to identify his vessels.

Some authorities have drawn attention to the frequency with which a seagull hovering over a piece of driftwood occurs in his paintings, and have suggested

Duncan McFarlane, *The Packet Antarctic*, signed and dated 1853, 61 x 92 cm. This portrait of the American-owned *Antarctic* demonstrates the fine draughtsmanship that typifies McFarlane's work. (National Maritime Museums, Greenwich, London)

this as a possible trademark. However, such a detail is often employed by a range of other artists and should be regarded with caution in making an attribution. It was one of the reasons for attributing the painting of *James T Foord and Miracle* to McFarlane, which has since been established to have almost certainly come from the hand of Francis Hustwick.

In addition to his oils, McFarlane seems to have produced a number of ship portraits in watercolour, perhaps to offer a less expensive option for those of more modest means. Of the surviving dozen or so examples, all completed for the American market, none are signed, perhaps indicating that he did not wish to draw overt attention to these and thus undercut himself.

There are good examples in the NMM, PEM and Mystic Seaport.

Lit.: Davidson 1986: 79–82; Davidson 1995: 20; Finamore 1995: 59–61, 64–65, 68–69; Tibbles 1999: 157–58; Wright et al. 2006: 544.

W. K. McMinn *The Duke off St Helena*, signed and dated 1845, 41 x 64 cm. *The Duke* is shown in two views off the unusual background of St Helena in the South Atlantic, in McMinn's easily recognisable style. (NML/MMM)

W. K. McMinn (1817–1898)

Although McMinn described himself as a 'marine painter' for much of his adult life, he almost certainly falls into the category of the 'artisan artist' who had another occupation, and we know that in later years he was undertaking work as a draughtsman. He had served as a mariner in his youth and brought this experience to bear on his artistic endeavours.

William Kimmins McMinn was born in Workington in 1817, the son of a block-maker, James McMinn, and his wife Sarah, and was baptised in the Presbyterian Chapel there on 13 April 1817. By April 1841 he was living with his elder brother, Peter, and his family in Toxteth Park, Liverpool, and both give their occupations as mariners. However, by the time he came to marry Catherine Simnor on 6 October that year at Christchurch, Liverpool, he was describing himself as 'artist', perhaps having left the sea as many men did on marrying. He and his wife seem to have moved in with her widowed father, William, who was a master porter, at 29 Horatio Street. McMinn exhibited a *Mersey Scene* at the Liverpool Academy in 1842. By 1851 his father-in-law had died and they were living at that same address with a growing family – Thomas, aged 9, Sarah, 6, and William, 1. Each of the children had been baptised at St Nicholas's Parish Church, and on each occasion McMinn was described as 'marine painter'. They had moved to Robert Street North by 1853 and to 48 Kensington by 1858, when he exhibited two paintings of pilot boats at the Liverpool Academy. He was still living there with his wife, three sons and two daughters, aged 19 to 3 years old, in 1861. McMinn was listed as a 'marine painter and draughtsman', a description which also appears in the local directories from 1862. In 1871 when McMinn was living in Field Street, Everton, he described himself as a 'marine painter' only. All his children, except William who had married the previous year, were single and living at home, though the family had also taken in a lodger.

By 1881 McMinn's wife Catherine and his eldest son, Thomas, were both dead. He was living with his three unmarried children, together with a niece from Ireland, at 23 Newlands Street, Everton. He had probably all but given up painting by this stage. His last known dated painting is the barque *Zelica*, signed and dated 1875, and McMinn himself is described in the census as a 'mechanical craftsman'. There is no reference to his being an artist and the local directories in 1886 and 1887 describe him only as a draughtsman. The same is true in 1891 when he is listed as 'a draughtsman general'. By this time only his daughter Catherine, a school teacher, was still living with him at 1 Aughton Street, Everton.

McMinn died on 2 July 1898, when his age was given as 80. He was then living with his eldest daughter, Sarah, at 42 Albion Street, Everton.

The majority of McMinn's known and dated paintings were completed in the 1850s and early 1860s. They bear testimony to his skill as a draughtsman with their careful depiction of the complex array of spars and rigging of the large sailing ships of the period. His technical ability is also corroborated by two surviving scale drawings of hull profiles and rigging (PEM). He is very good at depicting topographical details, such as the Liverpool waterfront in the portrait of the *James Langton* or the view of the paddle steamer *Leinster Lass*, where he accurately portrays the dog-leg channel leading into Drogheda in Ireland. One of his most unusual works is the view of the barque *Margaret Longton* shown at anchor in the Mersey. This must be one of the few ship portraits showing all sails neatly stowed. Every spar and the detail of the rig are faithfully portrayed and show the orderly complexity of the rigger's art and skill. He no doubt drew on his early experience of being a seafarer and also family connections. His elder brother, Peter, was an experienced mariner, gaining his master's certificate in 1851 just a year before he fell to his death from the rigging of the *Aeolus* off the Moroccan coast, and his youngest son, James, born in 1852, was later to become a rigger and mariner.

There are approximately twenty known works, with good examples in MMM and PEM.

Lit.: Davidson 1986: 82–84; Davidson 1995: 20–21; Finamore 1995: 50; Morris and Roberts 1998: 408; Tibbles 1999: 159–61; Wright et al. 2006: 548.

Henry Melling (1808–1879)

Henry Melling is probably best described as a gentleman artist, producing many hundreds of paintings, most of which seem to have remained in his possession until he died. He produced some memorable local maritime-related oils but also undertook historically inspired paintings and other works. He was a founder member of the Royal Mersey Yacht Club and served as its secretary for thirty-five years.

Melling was born in Sparling Street, Liverpool, in 1808, the son of Edward Melling and his wife Sarah. Edward Melling was a merchant and his wife was the sister of Egerton Smith (1774–1841), founder of the *Liverpool Mercury*. As a young man Melling had 'a great taste for the stage', but he preferred to study painting, enrolling at the Liverpool Academy. Perhaps it is no coincidence that in 1827 his painting *An English Coaster*, on show in the Academy's fourth exhibition, attracted the attentions of his uncle's *Mercury* which commented that he had 'a decided talent'.[1] He was to be a regular exhibitor over the next thirty years. In 1829 he moved to London where he studied art for a couple of years.

Melling returned to the family home in Kent Square and seems to have worked for a time with his brother, Edward. The family was involved with a number of enterprises. Edward trained as a shipbuilder and was working as such on his own account in 1828 and designing ships in the 1830s. He was appointed Superintendent of Naval Architecture at Liverpool Collegiate Institution in 1843. However, he was also involved with his brother-in-law, George Patmore Payne, in a printing and stationers' business and in providing 'optical, mathematical and navigational instruments'. Melling appears to have tried his hand at each of these businesses, being recorded in the local directories between 1834 and 1843 as painter, but also stationer and on one occasion optician. He never married and lived with various members of his family throughout his adult life. In 1841 he was living in the family home in Kent Square with his elder brother, Edward, and his mother, Sarah. He is described as an artist. Not long after this, he seems to have given up any idea of other employment, but it is very unlikely that he made a living from selling paintings, and he was presumably supported by some family money or an annuity.

Melling had a passion for sailing and in 1844 was one of the founder members of the Royal Mersey Yacht Club, and became its first honorary secretary, a post he held until his death. Membership of the club grew rapidly and in addition to races and regattas, it organised group cruises and provided escorts for visiting royalty and dignitaries. Melling himself owned a number of yachts over the years including *Seagull*, the 12-ton *Gem* and *Water Spirit*.

In 1847 and 1849 he was living in South Street, Toxteth Park, but by 1851 he was with his mother in Hemer Terrace, Bootle, when he is described as artist and honorary secretary of the Yacht Club. His mother died in September 1855 and he went to live with his sister, Harriette, the widow of optician George Patmore Payne, and her three daughters at 5 Alfred Street, Toxteth. In the early 1860s they moved to Quay House, Little Neston, where Harriette died in May 1867. He was living there with his niece, Harriette Melling Lloyd, and her two children in 1871, though her husband was not at home. At this stage he describes himself as 'artist, historical'. Melling is said to have left this house in about 1875 because of problems with sand in the estuary which was interfering with his yachting. He and the Lloyds moved to Gorad-y-Gyt, a house right on the Menai Straits near Bangor, where he died on 24 September 1879 at the age of 71. He left £1,100 to his niece. From about 1855 he had 'rooms', first in Duke Street and from about 1864 in Tower Buildings North, Water Street.

Melling was a prolific painter, and Edna Rideout writing in 1927 records having a catalogue listing his 'paintings in oils, watercolours, crayons, etchings, etc.' which were at Quay House in 1874.[2] According to his obituary, he left several hundred paintings in his studio when he died and bequeathed 250 of them to the Mayor and Corporation of Chester, 80 in trust to the magistrates of Bangor and some to the council in

---

1   *Liverpool Mercury*, 28 September 1827.

2   Rideout 1927: 155–56.

Henry Melling, *The Grand Regatta of the Royal Mersey Yacht Club*, 66 x 140 cm. Melling was an enthusiastic yachtsman, and yachts frequently feature in his paintings, either as the main subject, as here, or as a subsidiary element. (© Peter Nahum at The Leicester Galleries, London /Bridgeman Images)

Birkenhead.[1] It is not clear whether these bequests were carried out and what became of the paintings, but certainly there are relatively few in any public collections.

A number of his surviving maritime canvases are on a large scale, both physically and artistically, encompassing a large and varied scene with a wealth of different shipping. Examples are his *Liverpool Dock Scene and Warehouses* (WmAG) and *The Dry Bason* (MMM), showing the busy dock area at the entrance to the Old Dock. More modest works include yachting scenes, such as *Vision Winning the Mersey Yacht Club Grand Challenge Cup* of 1847, sold at Bonhams in 2015. Perhaps his

best-known painting is the *Wreck of the Ocean Monarch* (Royal Mersey Yacht Club), which shows the rescue attempt when this ship, taking emigrants to Boston, caught fire off the coast of North Wales in 1848.

Melling also undertook a large number of historical paintings. One of his first, *Retreat from Naseby*, was exhibited at the RA and was praised by Benjamin Haydon.[2] Other titles include *Caesar's Second Invasion* and *Prometheus and the Eagle*.

Lit.: Davidson 1986: 113; Morris and Roberts 1998: 424; Tibbles 1999: 161–62; Wright et al. 2006: 560.

---

1   *Liverpool Mercury*, 29 September 1879.

2   *Liverpool Mercury*, 29 September 1879.

Charles Ogilvy, *No.1 Pilot Schooner Queen*, signed and dated 1865, 29 x 47 cm. This is an excellent
example of Ogilvy's pilot boat paintings. (ARTUK/NML/MMM)

Charles Ogilvy (1832–1918)

Charles Ogilvy was a plumber and decorator, though from the late 1860s until the early 1890s he specifically referred to himself as an artist or marine artist. He is best known for his portraits of pilot vessels, which also feature in several of his other paintings.

Ogilvy was born in Liverpool in 1832 and was baptised at St Peter's Church on 22 May 1832. His parents were Thomas Ogilvy, a master mariner, probably originally from Lerwick in the Shetlands, and his wife Sarah, who lived in Chester Street, Toxteth. He was still living at home with his widowed mother and three siblings in Brunswick Street, Tranmere, in 1851, when the census recorded him as an 18-year-old plumber. In the 1854 directory he is in business as Ogilvy and Strettell, plumbers, painters and glaziers, with premises in Duke Street, though he appears to be still living with his mother, who had moved to Falkner Street. He described himself as 'plumber and painter' when he married Mary Ann Hodson on 20 July 1856. He gave his occupation as plumber when his eldest daughter was baptised in 1859, though by 1861 he is described by the more general title 'painter &c.'. Ogilvy and his wife were then living with their two young daughters at 7 Hutton Street, Everton.

Ogilvy is first listed as a 'marine artist' in *Gore's Directory* in 1868, and subsequently in a number of entries until 1884 at addresses corresponding to the census return.[1] He also described himself as 'artist' when his daughter Andrina was baptised in 1869, and as 'marine artist' in the 1871 census when they were living at 23 Orient Street, Everton.[2] In 1881, when he and his family of six children were living at 93 St John's Road, Everton, he gave his occupation as 'artist painter'. The 1891 census is again vaguer, describing him as 'painter', but when his daughter Frances married later that year his occupation was given specifically as marine artist. At the time of the census, they not only had four of their unmarried children living at home, but his married daughter Jessie and her husband Thomas Stubbs, a contractor's clerk, and two young grandchildren were also living with them. In the 1901 census, when they were living at 427 Hawthorne Road, Bootle, Ogilvy is described as 'Decorator / Paint / worker' and his 23-year-old son George, who was living at home, was also a painter.[3] By 1911 all the family had left home and Ogilvy and his wife were living on their own at 178 Gloucester Road, Bootle, and he was described as 'late occupation decorator'. The census also confirms that they had had nine children, though three of them were dead. Mary Ann died in December 1915 and Ogilvy himself died died on 30 November 1918, aged 87, and was buried in Kirkdale cemetery.

In 1986, of the four paintings by Ogilvy that were known, three were portraits of pilot schooners, and Davidson suggested that he might have been a mariner who had some connection with the pilot service. No documentary evidence for employment in the pilot service could be found, but Davidson pointed out that *Gore's Directory* for 1882 not only lists him as a marine painter in Orient Street, Everton, but that in the street list he is referred to as Charles Ogilvy mariner. However, this single reference is at odds with all the other information about him, and the most likely explanation is that this is a misprint on the part of the directory compilers. Overall the evidence suggests that his principal employment was as a painter and decorator, and we may conclude that whilst he tried to project and establish himself as a marine artist, this met with limited success.

Ogilvy clearly had a good knowledge of sailing vessels and their rigging, as the dozen or more paintings which have come to light in the last thirty years show a greater range of subjects and feature a number of fully rigged ships which are confidently and accurately portrayed. Ogilvy tends to use cool colours, with bright skies and a bluey-green sea that is often quite lively. Many of the works are signed and they date particularly from the late 1860s and early 1870s. They include a handful of

---

1   *Gore's Directory of Liverpool*, 1868, 1870, 1871, 1877, 1880, 1881 and 1884.
2   The census incorrectly gives their family name as O'Glery, but all the other details match other censuses and known information.
3   The census incorrectly gives their family name as O'Gilby.

paintings of American ships which have passed through the salerooms, such as the *Clipper Weighing Anchor off the Skerries* or the *American Ship St Joseph off Point Lynas*, both dated 1867. Several of them show a vessel calling for a pilot, such as the *Selina James* of 1868, or the *Sally*, 1870. It is worth noting that the connection with the pilot service remains, with virtually all of them depicted close to the pilot station at Point Lynas, off the North Wales coast, and several feature pilot vessels.

There are typical examples in MMM and Mystic Seaport, Connecticut.

Lit.: Davidson 1986: 86–87, 89; Tibbles 1999: 171–72; Wright et al. 2006: 612.

Philip Osment (1861–1947)

Philip Osment was a watercolourist who produced many coastal views and seascapes, as well as a range of landscapes. He was brought up in Liverpool and spent much of his adult life there, with probably protracted stays in North Wales, Scotland and Cornwall.

Osment was born in Exeter on 6 August 1861, the eldest son of Philip Daniel Osment, a silversmith, and his wife Sarah. Philip Daniel had inherited his father's well-established business in 1857 and was keen to develop it, advertising in April 1864 that he had 'recently erected new apparatus, on a larger scale than has ever been attempted in the West of England, for the purposes of electro-plating and gilding on the premises', thus negating the need to send items to Birmingham or Sheffield.[1] He was clearly overextending himself and in October the same year he was declared bankrupt. Even more tragically, he died the following spring, leaving his widow with two small sons.

Like many young women in similar circumstances, she seems to have come to an arrangement with a young widower, Reuben Tremlett, a local artist, who had been left with a young daughter, and they formed a relationship. Although no record of a marriage has been found, by 1871 they had moved to Liverpool and were living at 6 Phoebe Ann Street, Everton, as man and wife. In addition to her sons Philip and John, and his daughter Emily, they had a daughter, Marion, who was born in June 1869.

In 1881 the family was living at 24 George Street, Everton, and the 17-year-old Osment was described as an 'artistic student'. He left home shortly afterwards to live in lodgings, though not without incident. In January 1884 a notice appeared in the local paper stating that 'If Philip Osment, artist, does not call at 46 Lavan Street, within seven days, the articles belonging to him will be sold to pay expenses.'[2] He had no doubt done a runner!

Over the next twenty years, Osment seems to have spent a considerable amount of time in North Wales, as the 1891 census records him as 'landscape artist' living in Caerhun, in the Conway Valley, and in 1901 he was boarding with fellow landscape artist Peter Ghent (q.v.) and his family in Llanrhos, between Conway and Llandudno. Whether he was permanently resident in North Wales is not clear, and by 1909 he had returned to Liverpool and was living at 25 Freehold Street, Fairfield, and had a studio at 18 Chapel Street. Two years later, at the time of the census, he was living with his widowed mother and only surviving sibling, Marion. He described himself as an 'artist, (photographic)'. Marion was listed as a 'photographic retoucher'.

In 1921 Osment was described as a 'landscape artist' living at 4 Pennsylvania Avenue, Old Swan, with his mother, and after she died in 1923 he is intermittently listed there as an artist from 1924 to 1938. By September 1939 Osment, then 78 and described as a 'retired landscape and marine artist', was living with his now-widowed sister Marion in Haig Road, New Alresford, in Hampshire. He died from cancer in his right foot on 24 May 1947 and is buried in the village churchyard.

Osment worked mainly in watercolour, producing many marine paintings, including seascapes and coastal scenes with titles such as *Breaking Waves*, which usually featured a variety of sailing vessels, particularly yachts. He completed a number of local views, including Ellesmere Port and the Manchester Ship Canal. He also produced general landscapes of countryside and village life, and more occasional subjects included views of the African desert.

There are no examples of Osment's marine work in public collections.

Lit.: Davidson 1986: 135.

---

1 *Exeter and Plymouth Gazette*, 8 April 1864.
2 *Liverpool Mercury*, 18 January 1884.

Joseph Parry (1756–1826)

Joseph Parry is principally known as a genre and por-trait artist who worked in Manchester in the early nineteenth century and has been dubbed 'The Father of Art in Manchester'.[1] However, he was born and ini-tially worked in Liverpool, and he produced a number of marine paintings throughout his career.

Parry was born on 6 May 1756, the second son of Benjamin Parry, who was a river pilot. Although Benjamin's surname is variously spelt Parry and Perry, there is no reason to doubt that they were one and the same person. Benjamin gained his pilot's licence in 1759, was master of the No. 6 pilot boat in 1771, and is last mentioned as the master of the new No. 6 boat *Friend's Goodwill* when it entered service in 1781.

Little is known of Joseph Parry's time in Liverpool. He married Esther Dunbovand at St Paul's Church on 26 January 1777, when his occupation was given as 'painter'. They had eight children, three of whom died in infancy. He exhibited four paintings in 1787 – two were 'sea-pieces' and two were scenes of Castle Street in Liverpool. He had moved to Manchester by August 1790, when his fifth son William was baptised at St Ann's Church. He might have felt that Manchester offered a better market for the domestic and genre scenes which he mainly pro-duced. In 1800 he was living in Higher Ardwick and was described as 'portrait and sea-piece painter'. The link with Liverpool was obviously maintained: Parry exhibited three works at the Liverpool Academy in 1810, including one entitled *View from George's Dock*. His son William returned to his father's native town and fol-lowed his grandfather's occupation by engaging in the pilot service. He became a master pilot and died in 1847.

Parry himself was certainly successful in his career in his adopted home. He died in May 1826 and *Cowdroy's Manchester Gazette* commented, 'As an artist his powers were extreme – he painted Portrait, Landscape, History and Domestic scenes – in the latter his pictures possess extraordinary merit.'

Only four works with a marine subject have currently been identified. Two of these were completed before he left Liverpool and two were undertaken in Manchester. His view of *A Liverpool Privateer Returning with a Prize*, which is signed 'Jo[s] Parry. Pinx. Liverpool/1781' (MMM), is in fact the earliest surviving Liverpool ship portrait which is dated. It is relatively simplistic, compared with his later work, particular in the depiction of the sea. The paint-ing entitled *Armed Sailing Ship Mentor* probably dates from around the same period, as it is not only similar stylistically, but the vessel depicted was lost in a gale off Newfoundland whilst returning from Jamaica in 1782.[2] The 400-ton *Mentor* was a well-known ship, having captured the French East Indiaman *Carnatic*, the richest prize ever seized by a Liverpool privateer, in 1778.[3] *Mentor* is shown in three views, the main port profile filling most of the canvas, with distant views of her in port quarter view to the left and in stern quarter view to the right. She is probably shown off the Wirral coast opposite Liverpool, with Wallasey Pool and Bidston lighthouse visible under her bowsprit.

Two marine paintings from Parry's Manchester period have also been identified, through the careful observation of Charles Omell. *The John Bull Dropping off her Pilot* is a mas-terly composition, not only depicting a number of vessels in various views but capturing the atmosphere of what was often a hostile environment. The other Manchester canvas, *The Hope of Liverpool Passing a Crowded Jetty on the Approaches to Liverpool*, dates from 1810 and shows a ferry boat prob-ably at the entrance to one of the docks.[4] It is a delightful composition, with real characters in the boat struggling with the currents and again a wonderfully atmospheric sea and sky. In these two later paintings Parry demonstrates that he has advanced beyond the formulaic ship portraits of his youth and of many of his contemporaries.

There are good examples of his genre work in Manchester Art Gallery, including several canvases depicting the Eccles Wakes.

Lit.: Burleigh 1991; *ODNB*; Morris and Roberts 1998: 466; Tibbles 1999: 172–73; Wright et al. 2006: 624.

---

1   *ODNB*.

2   Parker Gallery, *Catalogue*, 1980, no. 25.

3   Williams 2004: 239.

4   Sold at Christie's, 11 November 1999, lot 562, incorrectly attributed to nineteenth-century Continental school, under the inaccurate title *Running Out to Sea with the Guardship Beyond with Spectators on the Pier*.

Joseph Parry, *Liverpool Privateer Returning with a Prize*, signed and dated 1781, 62 x 99 cm. This is the earliest dated Liverpool ship portrait that is currently known. (NML/MMM)

W. W. F. Preston *Starling*, signed and dated 1889, 43 x 69 cm. Preston produced mainly standard portraits of vessels in profile at sea, of which this is a nice example. (North Lincolnshire Museum Service)

Walter Preston (1865–c. 1915/20)

Walter William Frederick Preston was a ship portraitist and marine artist, who worked in Hull in the 1880s before moving to Liverpool in about 1890, where he worked for the next decade or so. He was probably unable to make a sufficient living from painting and was operating as an art dealer by 1911.

Preston was born in Gravesend on 28 February 1865 to Frederick Preston, a general labourer, and his wife Mary Elizabeth. By 1871 the family was living in Shoreditch and Frederick was working as an iron dresser in a foundry. It seems that Preston moved to Hull in his late teens and married 20-year-old dressmaker Theresa Alice Brewster there in the summer of 1883. He was living in Collier Street and working as an artist when twin sons were born in March 1884. Two more sons were born between 1885 and 1888. Preston was doing sufficiently well to be able to employ a servant, and in April 1889 he advertised for 'a general servant, accustomed to children – Apply Preston artist, 37 Bond Street'.[1] By December they were living at 42 New George Street where, on the night of the third, the shop 'of Mr W W F Preston, artist' was destroyed by fire. The crying of one of the children raised the alarm and the family escaped unharmed. He was apparently insured for £650 and he might have used the capital to relocate to Liverpool.[2] By April 1891 they were living at 88 Park Road, Toxteth, and Preston gave his occupation as artist. They were still able to employ a servant. He appears in one local directory in 1895 under the listing for artist, when his address is given as 26A Argyle Street, Birkenhead.

By 1901 Preston had moved to 8 Irvine Drive, Lower Bebington, and gave his occupation as 'commission agent', a rather general and indeterminate term. He appears to have separated from his wife, as she was living with the two eldest sons in Red Rock Street, Fairfield, north Liverpool. The two youngest sons, now aged 15 and 14, were living with their father and Elizabeth Richardson, a 27-year-old housekeeper.

The 1911 census informs us that Preston was now a widower and living at 182 Addison Road, King's Heath, Birmingham, where he was working as an artist and art dealer. Also living at the same address was his youngest son, George Clarence, then 24 and working as an 'engineer or motor mechanic'. Housekeeper Elizabeth Richardson was still living with them. After 1911 the trail goes cold and it has not been possible to trace him further.

There are about two dozen surviving works, including a group of portraits of local steamer and pilot boats which seem to have been completed in Hull, some of which are signed and dated to the late 1880s. Nine examples are in the Maritime Museum, Hull, and three are with the North Lincolnshire Museums Service. They are fairly standard portraits of vessels at sea. Few surviving works were completed in Liverpool, the most impressive being *Liverpool in the Present Day*, an attractive view of the Liverpool landing stages with a variety of shipping in the river, dating from 1893 (MMM). The following year it was exhibited in the summer exhibition at York City Art Gallery, where it attracted attention.[3] Preston's last known dated work is *Meeting up with the Pilot*, from 1900.

Lit.: Davidson 1986: 136; Tibbles 1999: 177–78; Wright 2006: 650.

---

1   *Hull Daily Mail*, 23 April 1889.
2   *Hull Daily Mail*, 3 December 1889.

---

3   *York Herald*, 12 July 1894.

'The Ribbon Artist'

The nickname 'The Ribbon Artist' has been given to an unidentified artist who was responsible for a group of ship portraits which not only feature characteristic name ribbons in the sky but are clearly in a consistent artistic style and are almost certainly by the same hand.

The artist is firmly in the tradition of folk art and stands aside from the other marine painters who were active in Liverpool at the time. His paintings have uniform seas with stylised foreground waves, which become just a flick of white paint in the middle and far distance, and his background locations are often crudely rendered. Equally memorable are his stick-like figures, which although rather two-dimensional, have a certain charm and are realistically deployed around the decks and in the yards. Despite the naivety of style, the vessels themselves are depicted with considerable accuracy and display a familiarity with ship construction and rigging.

Although only a small number of paintings are known, they cover an unusual breadth of subject matter including merchant and naval vessels, and some more specialist vessels such as a whaler and a pilot boat. All the paintings follow a standard formula, with the main subject placed in the centre in a broadside view and, ignoring perspective, usually showing the stern as well.

In each case, the vessel virtually fills the canvas and there is generally a hint of land in the background. In the sky, on either side of the vessel, the characteristic ribbons give the name and varying details of the vessel or its home port. A particularly interesting example is *Success to the James of Liverpool* (MMM), which shows an active whaling scene. The *James* is centre stage surrounded by ice floes, a line of whales and four longboats, some with harpoonists standing in the bow. A group of men are standing on a large ice floe killing a seal and four other vessels from the fleet are shown in the distance.

It seems likely that the artist was living or working in Liverpool in the first quarter of the nineteenth century. The majority of the vessels shown have some connection with Liverpool – being built, registered or regularly visiting the port – and most of the background locations are recognisable from local landmarks in the Mersey or along the North Wales coast, or will bear that interpretation. In terms of date, the operational lives of the vessels span a period of about sixty years from 1783, with a concentration of activity from about 1800 to about 1820/25.

There are four examples of his work in MMM.

Lit.: Davidson 1992: 8; Tibbles 1999: 152–56; Wright et al. 2006: 179.

'The Ribbon Artist', *Success to the James of Liverpool*, 57 x 86 cm. This characteristically naive painting, with its distinctive ribbon inscription, shows the *James* off Greenland and provides intimate detail of a whaler and her crew at work. (NML/MMM)

Walter Richards (1864–1926)

Walter Howard Richards was a lithographer who is known for one major oil painting, a panorama of Liverpool dating from 1907.

Richards was born in Kentish Town, London, in the early summer of 1864 to Joseph Thomas Richards, a draper, and his wife Emma. The family was living at 10 Kelly Street, Kentish Town, in 1871, but had moved to Liverpool by 1881, perhaps because his mother was originally from there. They were living at 18 Peet Street, off Edge Hill, and the 16-year-old Richards is described in the census as a lithographer. By 1891 they had moved to nearby Nuttall Street, and Richards was

described as a 'lithographic writer'. Three years later, *Kelly's Directory* recorded that he was in partnership with William Alderson as lithographic writers, with premises in Clarence Buildings, 40 North John Street.

Richards married Phoebe Hughes, the daughter of a bookkeeper, at St James's, New Brighton, on 17 August 1898, and they had two sons, one of whom died in infancy. In 1901 they were living at 64 Claremont Road, Wavertree, when Richards was described as 'lithographic writer and illuminating artist'. They moved to 9 Hawarden Road, Liscard, about 1905/06, and in 1911 Richards gave his occupation as 'artist, designer, lithographer'. He was described as an 'illuminator and etcher'

Walter Richards, *Modern Liverpool*, signed, 61 x 173 cm. This bird's-eye view of Liverpool captures the city in 1907 at the height of its fame as a global port. (NML/MMM)

when he produced an illuminated address which was presented to a local dignitary in 1919.[1] They were still living in Liscard in 1921, and he died there in the last quarter of 1926.

The only significant known work by Richards is *Modern Liverpool*, 1907 (MMM), a large bird's-eye view of the city from a vantage point south-west of the landing stage. It is very detailed, in an almost miniaturist manner, perhaps reflecting his skills as an illuminator, and not only features the main landmarks of the day but buildings throughout the city. In 1908 the *Liverpool Daily Post* offered large-scale colour reproductions of the painting at one shilling a piece and photogravure versions at a guinea.[2] An etching of the *Lusitania* at the landing stage in 1907 is the only work that has passed through the salerooms in recent years, and no other work by him has come to light.

---

1   *Birkenhead News*, 16 April 1919.

2   *Liverpool Echo*, 4 July 1908.

Dorothy Rimmer (1875–1951)

Dorothy Rimmer was a gifted amateur artist who is known for a handful of atmospheric marine views.

Rimmer was born in Liverpool on 10 May 1875, the daughter of Samuel Rimmer, a timber merchant, and his wife Clarissa (née Jones). The family moved to Woolton in the late 1870s, living first at Mount Aveline and then at Winwood Hall. Rimmer spent some time studying art in Paris. She was closely involved with the Woolton Flower Show during the First World War and after.[1] In 1921 she was living with her brother, Geoffrey, vicar of Helmsley in Yorkshire. When he moved to The Bolling, Malpas, in Cheshire shortly afterwards, she moved into the adjoining cottage, where she was still living in 1939. She was listed in the census as 'artist, private means' and died there on 15 August 1951, leaving £20,700.

Rimmer's views of the Mersey, including *SS Marwarri* and *The Mersey* (both MMM), give a good impression of the river in wartime. She had a very atmospheric and impressionist style but she also accurately portrayed the shipping, and her backgrounds are clearly recognisable. Other similar scenes occasionally feature at auctions.

Lit.: Tibbles 1999: 178–80.

---

1   *Runcorn Weekly News*, 4 July 1913, 16 July 1915, 25 July 1924.

Dorothy Rimmer, *Marwarri*, signed and dated 1940, 50 x 64 cm. The Brocklebank-owned *Marwarri* was requisitioned during the Second World War and is depicted in a view from Rimmer's office in the Cunard building. (ARTUK/NML/MMM)

Odin Rosenvinge (1880–1959)

Odin Rosenvinge is best known for the series of bold and colourful posters he produced for many of the major liner companies during the first half of the twentieth century. In particular, he was responsible for some of the most iconic images of Cunard liners, including *Lusitania*, *Aquitania* and *Berengaria*.

Rosenvinge was born in North Shields, on the outskirts of Newcastle upon Tyne, on 18 August 1880. His father Christen had been born in Ringkjobing, Denmark, in 1852/53, but had moved to Newcastle in the early 1870s, and on 3 May 1877 he married Clara Oliver, a local seamstress. In 1881 they were living in North View, Heaton, closer to the centre of Newcastle, and Christen gave his occupation as a ship broker's clerk. Ten years later Christen had progressed substantially and was himself a ship's broker, living with his growing family in the heart of the city.

In 1901 when Rosenvinge was 20, he was still at home in Rye Hill, Newcastle, and his occupation is given as a steel manufacturer's clerk. Davidson knew Rosenvinge's son Olaf, who provided additional information about his father's early career. As a young boy, Rosenvinge was fond of sketching and drawing, and for a time he worked as a court reporter, embellishing his articles with quick sketches. He clearly wanted an artistic career, and shortly afterwards obtained a job as an illustrator with a printing firm in Leeds. He might have been working there when he produced a shipping image for a commemorative address presented to Edward VII during a visit to Manchester in 1905.[1]

In 1907 he married Mildred Unwin in Newcastle, and by the time their first son Erik was born twelve months later they were living in the Crosby area, north of Liverpool. In 1911 their address was given as Carrs Crescent, Formby, and his occupation as an artist with a colour printer. Soon afterwards they moved to the Wirral, where they lived for the rest of their lives. The move to Liverpool was probably to take up a job with Turner & Dunnett, the printing company which produced posters and other advertising material for many of the major shipping companies. Some of Rosenvinge's earliest work was to promote the *Lusitania* (1907) and other Cunard vessels. He was to work for the printing firm for more than twenty years, latterly as chief artist.

When war came in 1914, Rosenvinge continued to work for Turner & Dunnett and was responsible for at least two of the official recruiting posters, 'He's happy and satisfied, are you?' and 'Make us proud', both issued in 1915. However, he clearly wanted to make a more direct contribution to the war effort and joined the Army Service Corps, serving as a private in the Middle East and taking part in the Palestine Campaign. He found time to do some drawing and painting, including watercolours of the *Tomb of the Virgin Mary in Jerusalem* and a landscape of *Medjel Yaba*, where the Turkish army was routed in September 1918.

In 1921 Rosenvinge was living at 4 Browning Avenue, Rock Ferry, with his wife, two sons, Erik and Olaf, and a daughter, Mildred. He had returned to his position with Turner & Dunnett, but over the following years strained trading conditions found the firm in difficulties. According to Davidson it went into liquidation in the early 1930s and Rosenvinge found himself without a job. Exactly what happened is not clear, but the firm was certainly still trading in the late 1930s and early 1940s, perhaps having been reformed and refinanced. Rosenvinge turned freelance and although he continued to do maritime-related work, he also broadened his range to cover other subjects.

By 1938 he had premises in Chapel Street in the centre of Liverpool, and in September 1939 he, his wife, son Olaf and daughter Mildred were still living in Browning Avenue, his occupation listed as a 'commercial artist (marine)'. During these years he also entered works into the annual Autumn Exhibitions at the Walker Art Gallery, his subjects including landscape and continental views as well as his more normal maritime subjects. Rosenvinge was still living in Browning Avenue when he died on 4 September 1959, leaving £466.

A number of museums hold copies of his posters and other promotional work, including MMM, NMM, Glasgow Museums, Southampton Museums and the Imperial War Museum. A few oil paintings

---

1   *Manchester Courier and Lancashire General Advertiser*, 12 July 1905.

survive, including the Cunarder *Tuscania* in Glasgow, and WmAG has a landscape of a waterfall entitled *The Kingfisher*. His posters frequently appear in auctions on both sides of the Atlantic.

Rosenvinge's younger son Olaf (1913–2005) was also a professional artist, producing literary-inspired landscapes, often with figures in a free style and verging towards fantasy. There is a selection of his work in WmAG.

Lit.: Davidson 1986: 117–19, 124.

Odin Rosenvinge, *Cunard Line*, 110 x 62 cm. This poster for Cunard, dating from the 1920s, is typical of the bold images used by Rosenvinge. (Shawshots/Alamy Stock Photo)

Robert Salmon (1775–c. 1845)

Robert Salmon's name is closely associated with Liverpool and he is recognised as one of the most talented marine painters to have worked in the town. However, he only spent two relatively short periods in the port. He first came to Liverpool in June 1806 and stayed until April 1811. Just over a decade later he returned for a briefer sojourn, arriving in October 1822 and leaving at some time in 1825. He spent much of his working life elsewhere, particularly in Greenock and in Boston, Massachusetts, where he is generally credited with making a major contribution to the development of American marine painting.

Salmon has attracted considerable scholarly attention. John Wilmerding produced a monograph on the artist in 1971, which provides an excellent general survey and is particularly informative about his years in Boston.[1] This is partly because he was well known there during his own lifetime but also because a transcript of a notebook he kept from 1806 has survived and was published by Wilmerding. The entries in the notebook are sparse until his arrival in America in 1828, when he started recording information about each individual painting as he completed and sold it. More recently, Davidson has considered in detail his Greenock years as well as adding information about his final years.[2] In these present remarks, greatest attention is given to Salmon's time in Liverpool and to his paintings that feature the port and its locality.

Although he is now generally known as Salmon, he was born Salomon and only adopted the shortened name on a regular basis in middle age. Indeed, he is sometimes referred to in contemporaneous documents as Solomon or Solloman. Whether his adopted name was an attempt to disguise his almost certain Jewish ancestry must remain speculation, but this is the likeliest explanation. Other members of his family also made this change in due course.

Robert Salmon was born in Whitehaven, the second son of Francis and Susannah Salomon. He was baptised at St James's Parish Church on 5 November 1775. In *The Cumberland Pacquet* of 1 December 1774, Francis had advertised himself as a working silversmith who had moved from London and recently established a shop in King Street. It seems almost certain that Francis was originally a Jew, but he seems to have abjured the faith by the time he arrived in Whitehaven, as his children were all baptised in the Anglican church there. He might still have been part of the small Jewish community in the town on a social basis.

Nothing is known of Salmon's education but it seems likely that he had some practical instruction in painting, though no details have been found. His earliest known paintings date from 1800, and although they feature ships off Whitehaven, they might have been completed after he left the town. By 1802 when he exhibited at the RA he was living in London, and he is presumed to have remained there until his move to Liverpool in 1806.

According to the transcript of his notebook, Salmon arrived in Liverpool on 10 June 1806 with the not insignificant sum of 26 guineas. Despite remaining for five years, there do not appear to be any references to him locally, not even in the street directories. We do, however, have the evidence of about 25–30 surviving paintings from this period (though they represent less than a quarter of the 113 which we know from his notebook that he completed in the town). His notes tell us that his first Liverpool picture was a now untraced *The Battle of Trafalgar*, painted speculatively but which he sold for 8 guineas. He also completed three paintings, which do survive, marking the visit to Liverpool of the Prince of Wales in September 1806. These include a view of the illuminations at the Town Hall (WAG) and two versions of the Prince's visit to the docks (Portland Museum of Art, Maine, and Private Collection, US). Another painting with a royal connection is the untraced *The Lady Warburton in the River Plate*, which he records in his notes as being completed in 1809 for Sir John Warburton to present to the Prince of Wales. The charge of 18 guineas is a significant sum and no doubt qualified it for inclusion amongst a small number he listed under the heading 'Special Pictures'. Information about his other Liverpool paintings is not recorded.

---

1   Wilmerding 1997.
2   Davidson 2001.

Robert Salmon, *View of the Mersey, 1807*, signed with initials and dated 1807, 51 x 78 cm. Dating from Salmon's first stay in Liverpool, this painting features an unknown ship in two views off the waterfront. (ARTUK/NML/WAG)

Salmon left Liverpool in April 1811 for Greenock and was to spend the next eleven years of his life on the banks of the Clyde. He returned to Liverpool on 11 October 1822 and stayed until the summer of 1825. Some corroboration exists for his time in the town. He exhibited five paintings at the Liverpool Academy in 1824. His address is given in the catalogue as 'North Shore', though the street directories of the same year list him as 'R Solomon Warwick Street, Toxteth'.

The works exhibited at the Academy included:

15	*An English Merchantman*
19	*Dumbarton*
20	*Greenock*
123	*A Pleasure Yacht*
128	*Stiff Breeze off the Ayrshire Coast*
154	*Fire at Wapping*

It is not now possible to identify these paintings from such brief and general descriptions, but it is interesting that at least three of them have Scottish connections. It seems to be typical of Salmon that he both kept paintings in stock which travelled with him and that he did not limit himself to the locality where he resided. It is thus a reminder that whilst most paintings with a Liverpool or Mersey background were painted during his time in the town, that is not necessarily the case, and some significant locally related works were completed in Greenock and Boston.

During this second period in Liverpool Salmon completed about eighty paintings. Whilst some of these were clearly for local patrons, his notes tell us that a handful were sold, almost certainly at a later date, at auctions in London and Bristol.

Robert Salmon, *American Ships in the Mersey off Liverpool*, signed with initials, 42 x 61 cm. This is probably one of the last paintings that Salmon undertook before leaving England for the last time, perhaps completed in the days before he departed for America. (NML/WAG)

Robert Salmon, *The Brig St Lucia in the Mersey*, signed with initials and dated 1821, 51 x 79 cm. This is a perfect example of the craftsmanship Salmon deployed in his portraits – an accurate and detailed profile of the vessel with a secondary view, his characteristically scalloped sea, a precise and accurate depiction of the background and interesting subsidiary activity on the river. (ARTUK/NML/MMM)

After Salmon left Liverpool in the summer of 1825, he began a period of extensive travel and does not seem to have settled for long in one place. He spent time in Greenock, London, Southampton, the north-east (including Newcastle and South Shields) and the south-west (Devon, Cornwall and Bristol). This peripatetic existence was only brought to an end when, on 16 June 1828, he sailed from Liverpool for New York, travelling on to Boston, where he arrived on 14 August. There is no indication as to why, in his early fifties, he made this change. It is clear from his notebook that he took a significant number of paintings with him. What is perhaps more surprising is that on arriving in Boston he did not immediately begin any commissions. Indeed, to judge from his notes, he spent most of his first nine months in the town painting things 'for selff', apart from one view of Boston and a 'drop sean' for the theatre. The impression is that this was from choice and that he was financially secure.

Salmon remained in Boston for more than a decade and established a formidable reputation as a marine artist. In 1842 the *Boston Daily Advertiser* commented, 'As a marine Painter, Mr Salmon has never been excelled by any artist in this country.' Not surprisingly, the majority of his output was of local subjects, but his notebook records four Liverpool-related subjects, including the *View of Liverpool from Cheshire*, completed in January 1840 and now in PEM.

Salmon's last years are shrouded in mystery. Entries in his notebook stop in July 1840, and in the same month a notice in the *Boston Daily Advertiser* of a sale of more than seventy paintings by him includes the statement that this will be his last sale, 'his physician having forbidden him to paint any small work'. Two years later in June 1842, the *Advertiser* reported that he 'has returned to Europe'. However, attempts to discover his destination have proved unsuccessful. Several paintings, apparently in Salmon's hand, survive from the period 1841–43, mainly in American collections. They are signed with his usual initials R S but are followed by either A T or M T, possibly suggesting a collaborator. More intriguing are two Italian scenes, *View of Palermo* and *View of Venice*, both signed with the initials R S and dated 1845. They are not entirely characteristic of the artist and they do little to resolve the mystery of his final years. Even more perplexing is a more recent discovery of another painting signed and dated 'R S 1845'. This view, *A regatta on the Mersey in a Flat Calm*, is an unmistakable Salmon. It confirms that he was still alive in 1845 and was still capable of producing a fine and arresting work. But it allows us to draw no other significant conclusions. He is presumed to have died before 1851, when there is a comment in the *Boston Evening Transcript* that 'Since Salomon's death, we have no one, who can paint a ship and ocean prospect like him.' Unless, and until, further definite evidence merges, we will not know the full details of Salmon's final years.

Salmon's surviving paintings show why he was such a successful artist. He was a master of both composition and detail. He provides more than a mere portrait of a ship – he shows a realistic scenario in terms of what the vessel is doing and the other shipping and activity on the river. Although the majority of the vessels he depicts are not identified or are not now identifiable, they are generally shown in great detail and with an accuracy which must have made them immediately recognisable to the initiated at the time. Furthermore, he places them against actual locations, mostly in the Mersey, which are depicted in the finest detail and with great accuracy. They thus provide a marvellous topographical record, particularly of the Liverpool waterfront. The only potentially discordant note is his characteristically lifeless sea with its sculpted, almost regimented waves, which is unconvincing. Only on rare occasions did he deviate from this effect and he occasionally showed vessels in a more natural style, such as *Ship Liverpool in the Mersey*[1] or in a more turbulent sea such as *The Mail Packet from Liverpool to Glasgow*.[2]

In terms of composition the majority of his surviving paintings are variations on a theme – but no less appealing for that. The most common composition is that of *A Sailing Ship in the Mersey* of 1811 (WAG) or *The Brig St Lucia in the Mersey* of 1821 (MMM) – a central profile view

---

1   Sold at Phillips, London, 3 April 2001, lot 26.
2   Private collection, illustrated Wilmerding 1971: 36.

of the vessel and a secondary view or other vessel to the right, with a balancing vessel, often a small boat, astern against a background of the Liverpool waterfront looking north towards Garston. Variations have vessels at different stages of activity with appropriate displays of sail and a range of subsidiary shipping. Occasionally a straighter view of the waterfront is used as the background. In another group, Salmon uses the Wirral shore as the background but with similar compositional elements. Some details also appear regularly – a gig boat alongside the main vessel, a ferry boat or pilot boat in the distance.

At various times in his career, Salmon also produced a number of paintings which are not the traditional single-ship portrait but include a general view across the Mersey from the Wirral shore, with Liverpool in the distance and a wider variety of shipping, perhaps with one vessel more prominently depicted. The earliest of these, the previously mentioned *Ship Liverpool in the Mersey*, dates from 1810, but there are later examples such as *View of Liverpool* of 1825,[1] which includes a detailed view of the Wirral foreshore at Wallasey, and the very similar *View of Liverpool from Cheshire* (PEM), dating from 1840.

Salmon also undertook some topographical works which do not include any marine elements, such as the *Illumination of the Liverpool Town Hall* of 1806 (WAG), or the later *Bidston Old Lighthouse and Flagpoles* of 1825 (MMM).

He is represented in most of the major British and American maritime collections and his work frequently appears at auction.

Lit.: Wilmerding 1971; Hay 1979; Davidson 1986: 22–24; Davidson 1995: 15–16; Davidson 2001: 23–47; Finamore 1995: 39–41; Morris and Roberts 1998: 532; Tibbles 1999: 183–86; Wright et al. 2006: 700-01.

----

1   Illustrated Wilmerding 1971: 11.

J. T. Serres, *George's Dock Basin, Liverpool*, 46 x 61 cm. This is one of a small number of canvases with a local background that Serres produced during his time in Liverpool. (Photo © Bonhams, London, UK /Bridgeman Images)

John Thomas Serres (1759–1825)

John Thomas Serres was marine artist to George III for a number of years and travelled widely in England and abroad. He spent two or three years in Liverpool from about 1796 to 1799.

Serres was born in December 1759, the son of the French-born marine artist Dominic Serres (1722–93), who had come to England as a prisoner of war around 1758. He followed his father's profession and in 1790 travelled to Paris and Italy. He married his former pupil Olivia Wilmot in 1791 and they had two daughters, but it was not a happy marriage and they formally separated in 1804. He was working as a marine draughtsman at the Admiralty in 1800 and was a drawing instructor at the Chelsea Naval School. Serres was dogged by financial difficulties in his later years, being imprisoned for debt in Edinburgh in 1818, and he died in the debtors' prison in London in 1825.

During his time in Liverpool Serres stayed with the engraver and artist Moses Haughton the Younger (1773–1849). His painting of *Earl Howe's naval victory of the Glorious First of June*, 1794, and other naval paintings were exhibited at the Exchange Hall in May 1796. The following year he published *Four Views of Liverpool*, which were available by subscription for five guineas. He also completed the impressive canvas *The Pearl Frigate off Liverpool*, which is now at Waddesdon Manor. A number of drawings of ships and local landmarks, and a sketchbook of views of Seacombe and Woodside, dating from October 1796 to March 1797, are in LCL. *A View of Woodside, Birkenhead* of 1799 is in WmAG.

There are several examples of his marine paintings in NMM, and works in WmAG, WAG, the V&A, the Science Museum, NMW, the Royal Collection, Government Art Collection and in several National Trust properties.

Lit.: *ODNB*; Wright et al. 2006: 713.

John Shimmin (1933–)

John Shimmin was born in 1933 in West Derby and continued to live in the area. He studied briefly at the Liverpool School of Art before stowing away on a Blue Funnel liner aged 15. As well as serving time in the Merchant Navy, he was also a soldier, delivery man, debt collector, air steward, freelance cartoonist and taxi driver.[1]

Shimmin produced over 200 paintings, mainly ship portraits in the Mersey, holding shows at the Neptune Gallery in 1975 and the Davey Gallery in 1984. He exhibited at the Liverpool Academy of Arts and the Royal Society of Marine Artists.[2] He designed a monument to Merchant Navy seamen that was unveiled on the Pier Head by the then Deputy Prime Minister, John Prescott, in 1998.[3]

---

1 *Liverpool Echo*, 20 May 1975, 15 November 1989.

2 *Liverpool Echo*, 20 May 1975, 9 June 1984.
3 *Liverpool Echo*, 24 September 1998.

Max Sinclair, *In the Mersey*, signed and dated 1889, 115 x 183 cm. This evocative scene of a variety of shipping off the Liverpool waterfront is typical of Sinclair's atmospheric paintings. (NML/MMM)

Max Sinclair (Max Krause, 1861–1931)

Max Sinclair is probably the most mysterious of all the artists who worked in Liverpool in the late nineteenth century. Although he is frequently mentioned as a landscape and marine artist in newspapers of the 1880s and 1890s, and a significant number of his works survive, no biographical details have been found that relate to anyone of this name, and it seems most likely that 'Max Sinclair' was a pseudonym for Max Krause.[1]

The grounds for making this suggestion are that 'Sinclair' is referred to in 1880 as 'the gifted pupil' of Franz Emil Krause (1836–1900), a landscape artist who became a naturalised British citizen.[2] The 1881 census includes Francis Krause, a landscape artist born in Berlin who was living in Manchester with his wife Amelia and six children, the eldest of whom was Max Krause, aged 20, and listed as 'artist, marine painter'. This would tie in with other newspapers reports in which 'Sinclair' is referred to on one occasion as 'of Manchester' and on another as 'a young North of England artist'.[3] His youth is also commented upon on other occasions – in 1881 he was described as 'this gifted young man' and in 1888 as an artist who 'is making steady progress and his works are finding great favour with the leading collectors'.[4] Comparison of the surviving paintings of Krause senior and 'Sinclair' shows an uncanny similarity. It may be that he thought he would have more critical and commercial success as a 'British' rather than a 'foreign' artist. A small number of marine paintings signed 'M. Krause' also survive, and show considerable similarities to works signed Sinclair, especially in the handling of the sea and the overall atmospheric style. There are also occasional contemporary references to paintings by Max Krause.[5] To add to the mystery, there are several landscapes in watercolour in the collections of Manx National Heritage which are signed 'M. Crouse'. Krause's death certificate confirms that he used both names, referring to him as 'Henry Max Crouse otherwise Krause'.

Heinrich [Henry] Max Krause was born in Berlin on 2 March 1861 to Franz Krause, a landscape artist, and his wife Amelie. His parents and family moved to England, settling in Manchester in 1878.[6] He started exhibiting his work from 1880 onwards but was clearly still studying. In 1883 he was given a commendation of 'excellent' in the examination of 'Advanced Art-Perspective' at the Manchester Technical School and Mechanics Institution.[7] He married Mary Jane Mansell on 20 May 1885 in Manchester, and in 1891 they were lodging at 102 Stanhope Street in Toxteth, with a widowed schoolmistress. Although his name is given as Crowse and his place of birth is given as Iowa, USA, all the other details regarding him and his wife tally, including his occupation as an artist. By 1901 they were living back in Manchester, at 49 Perth Street, near Cheetham Hill, and though there appears to be another variation in his name, the census listing him as Frederick Max Crause, again all the other details of birth, age and occupation agree. In 1911 they were living in Ashleigh, Dane Road, Sale, and he continued to give his occupation as artist.

A further reference to the couple comes in October 1916 when they found themselves in court. Apparently, Krause was unable to claim British nationality along with his parents and siblings in 1887 because of his age, and thus he remained a German citizen. He had registered his residence in Southport with the authorities in 1914, claiming, perhaps inaccurately, that he had lived there 'on and off for the past thirty years …

---

1 Other researchers have independently come to the same conclusion; see https://www.artuk.org/artdetective/discussions/discussions/can-we-establish-if-max-sinclair-and-max-crouse-are-the-same-artist.

2 *Aberdeen Free Press*, 30 September 1880.

3 *Northern Whig*, 20 September 1886; *Eastbourne Gazette*, 18 September 1889.

4 *Hampshire Telegraph*, 10 August 1881; *South Wales Daily News*, 17 May 1888.

---

5 *Sheffield Independent*, 15 August 1884, refers to the oil painting of Dublin Custom House; *Derbyshire Advertiser and Journal*, 3 October 1890, comments on 'an admirable picture of big ships unloading "Our Food Supply"'.

6 *Liverpool Weekly Courier*, 16 February 1889.

7 *Manchester Courier and Lancashire General Advertiser*, 1 August 1883.

and continuously for the last four or five years'.[1] The town was in a restricted area and he was told to move to Salford, but was sent back and forth between the two until he was charged with entering a prohibited area without a licence. The case was resolved when the couple moved to Staffordshire.[2] They clearly returned to Lancashire after the war and were living at 197 Portland Street, Southport, in 1921. He was still living there when he died of cancer of the bladder on 11 December 1931, his profession given as 'An Artist (Painter)'.

'Max Sinclair' is probably best known for three works featuring vessels in the Mersey, which are in the collections of MMM. They comprise a large and impressive view of *City of New York* and other shipping off the Liverpool waterfront and a pair of atmospheric views at the entrance to the Mersey. One other painting with a local subject is known and one or two others might possibly have a Merseyside connection. At least one painting features the port of London and others are set off Tynemouth, the Channel Islands and other unidentified ports and locations. Sinclair tended to give his paintings titles such as *Before Tripped Anchor* or *Running for Shelter*, and these are usually inscribed on the back of the canvas, often with a signature and occasionally a

date. He is known to have used a monogram (incorporating his two initials) on some occasions. Only a few of his ship paintings are in fact dated, from 1885 and 1887. However, judging by the vessels depicted, most of the canvases appear to have been completed during the 1880s.

The majority of Sinclair's marine works are very atmospheric and often feature highly dramatic effects, particularly in the sea and the sky. Some are set late in the day with long shadows and glistening seas, whilst others have a clearer but still rather portentous light. Whilst the vessels are clearly the subject, Sinclair appears to have been aiming for overall effect and sought to capture the wider context rather than producing a mere conventional ship portrait. Backgrounds are not generally painted with the same degree of detail, which often prevents precise identification.

Sinclair also painted landscapes, mainly of coastal scenes, and locations include North Wales, Scotland, Northumberland, Devon, the Channel Islands and the south coast. Again, many of these are inscribed and dated, mostly in the 1880s.[3] His younger brother was Emil Krause (q.v.).

Lit.: Tibbles 1999: 187–91; Wright et al. 2006: 726.

---

1   His parents were living in Southport in 1887 and in 1891; *Gore's Directory of Liverpool*, 1887; Census 1891.
2   *Liverpool Echo*, 6 October 1916; *Manchester Evening News*, 7 October 1916.

---

3   There is a painting of *Loch Goil* in the National Library of Wales, which has previously been dated [18]'64' but on close examination is actually dated [18]'84'.

Walter Thomas (1894-1962)

Walter Thomas is best known as the designer of shipping posters for two of Liverpool's foremost printing companies. He produced work for all the major shipping lines and in particular was responsible for nearly all the promotional material for Blue Funnel from the interwar years until the late 1950s.

Thomas was born on 24 June 1894, the son of Arthur R. Thomas, an accountant with the Mersey Docks and Harbour Board, and his wife Emily. In 1901 the family was living in Rosslyn Street, Toxteth, but by 1911 they had moved to Belgrave Road, Liscard. Davidson states

that Thomas trained as a naval architect and also worked on cataloguing Lord Leverhulme's art collection. At the time of the 1911 census, when he was 17, he was working as a lithographic designer for a printing company. This might have been Turner & Dunnett, where he was later assistant artist to Odin Rosenvinge (q.v.). In 1921 he was still living at home in Liscard and is described as 'artist and designer' working for J. Haworth & Bros., Printers. By 1927 he was chief artist at the Liverpool Printing Company. He married Nora Ellis in 1929 but they had no children. In September 1939 Thomas, his wife and his father-in-law, a retired printer, were living at 1 Redstone

Walter Thomas, *Perseus off Gibraltar*, signed, 53 x 72 cm. This is was of the few oil paintings produced by Thomas, and was commissioned for the offices of the Blue Funnel Line. (ARTUK/NML/MMM)

WALTER THOMAS

Close, Hoylake. Interestingly, Thomas gives his occupation as 'artist, marine and landscape, painter etc., maker of models in plaster, contour maps'. He had developed a special relationship with the Blue Funnel Line, and Sir Sydney Jones, a partner in the firm, recommended him as a camouflage artist to the Admiralty. After the end of the war he went freelance, with a contract to undertake all Blue Funnel requirements.

The family later moved to Loggerheads, near Mold in North Wales, and in 1948 Thomas became a member of the Royal Cambrian Academy. In the early 1950s they moved to the Isle of Man, and in addition to his freelance work, he also undertook commissions from the island's publicity department. He died in Kirk Michael, Isle of Man, on 9 April 1962, leaving £948 to his widow.

Like most poster artists, Thomas's work is characterised by bright, bold images, and he created some memorable examples of the genre. Over the course of his career, in addition to his Blue Funnel commissions, he produced work for most of the major shipping companies, but particularly Cunard, White Funnel,

Canadian Pacific and Elder Dempster. He occasionally produced oil paintings, such as *Glenroy in Camouflage* and *Perseus off Gibraltar* (both MMM).

Thomas also worked in Scotland. He painted a mural for the vestibule of the boardroom of the Caledon shipyard in Dundee and spent nine 'painstaking days' in a small boat making sketches and preliminary drawings for the commission. Perhaps unsurprisingly, the final work included a Blue Funnel liner in the fitting-out bay.[1] He provided a mural of one of the miracles of St Ninian for the coastal steamer of that name, built at Caledon in 1950, and he was employed in the design of the public rooms of the vessel.[2]

There are examples of his graphic work in MMM, NMM and other UK collections.

Lit.: Davidson 1986: 118, 138; Tibbles 1999: 193–94.

---

1   *Dundee Evening Telegraph*, 7 March 1950. The painting is now in the collections of Dundee Art Galleries and Museum (17-1989).
2   *Dundee Courier*, 7 March 1950.

Alfred Trant (1867–1934)

Alfred William Vincent Trant was a master mariner who came from a seafaring family and spent most of his career working for the Leyland Line. He seems to have dabbled as a painter on an amateur basis.

Trant was born in Liverpool in the spring of 1867, the son of Captain William Trant and his wife Mary. He went to sea as a ship's boy on SS *Drumpark*, sailing to Australia in 1883, and gained his second mate's certificate in 1886 and his master's ticket in 1890. He married Martha Sumner, the daughter of a veterinary surgeon, in April 1892 and they had three children. After she died in 1903, he married Ann Eliza Wannop in early 1905, and they had three more children. In 1911 he was at sea but the family was living at Aysgarth Avenue, West Derby.

Trant was captain of a number of Leyland Line vessels, including SS *Devonian*, on which he served for many years on the Liverpool to Boston route. He was involved in the rescue of crew and passengers from the emigrant ship *Volturno*, which caught fire in mid-Atlantic in October 1913.[1] *Devonian* was torpedoed by U-53 off the Donegal coast in August 1917. In November 1917 Trant was appointed as Marine Superintendent of the Mercantile Marine Division at the Admiralty.[2] After the war he resumed his career and in 1921 the family was living at Upton Park, Moston, on the Wirral. He later worked for the Red Star Line and retired in 1932. He died on 9 April 1934, leaving £4,300.

Trant's unsigned painting of SS *Drumpark* (MMM) bears a label recalling his first voyage. The other known work, *City of Sparta*, signed 'AWVT / 1908', is in the British Mercantile Marine Memorial collection.

Lit.: Tibbles 1999: 195.

_____

1   *Leeds Mercury*, 28 November 1913.
2   *Liverpool Daily Post*, 31 December 1917.

Herbert Trevethan (1910–1996)

Herbert Edgar Holt Trevethan was an amateur artist who won first prize with a maritime scene in the Wirral Spring Exhibition of 1984.

Trevethan was born in Llandudno on 29 August 1910 to Richard Trevethan, an electrical engineer's clerk, and his wife Ada. In 1911 the family was living in Chapel Street, Llandudno, but by 1921 they had moved to 29 Trafalgar Drive, Lower Bebington. Trevethan joined the Royal Regiment of Artillery in 1938, but had transferred by 1941 when he was sent for six months' aircrew training at the Naval Air Station in Grosse Ile, Michigan, USA.

Trevethan married Maureen Lightburn in 1943 in a ceremony on the Wirral, and lived locally for the rest of his life. He died on 3 April 1996.

His somewhat naive *The Mersey Remembered* won first prize in the Wirral Spring Exhibition in April 1984.

Charles J. Waldron (1835/36–1891)

Charles Waldron had a very successful painting and decorating business in Liverpool, employing nearly a dozen men, and appears to have been able to retire by the time he was in his early fifties. Only a handful of ship portraits by him are known – all completed for the American market – and ship portraiture was almost certainly a hobby rather than a second occupation for him.

Waldron was born in Ireland in 1835/36, but how and when he came to Liverpool remains a mystery. The earliest reference to him is when one of his apprentices fell and drowned whilst painting a ship in Stanley Dock in December 1862.[1] He is next listed in *Gore's Directory* in 1864 as a painter with premises at 21 Oil Street in the north of the town, not far from Waterloo Dock. He is listed in later directories as a 'paint and oil merchant' and 'oil and colour merchant', suggesting perhaps that he had expanded his business into providing other tradesmen, and probably ship owners and captains, with supplies of paint and oils. In the 1871 census he is listed as a master painter employing eight men and two boys, and he had ten men on his staff in 1881, which suggests that it was a significant business.

The electoral registers for Liverpool and Cheshire provide details from 1866 onwards. They give his residence first at 15 West Secombe Terrace, Poulton-cum-Seacombe, then from 1872 at number 17 in the same road; from 1884 until his death he lived at 78 Wheatland Road. They also confirm that he had a warehouse in Oil Street, Bootle, and from 1877 a shop at 67 Waterloo Road.

The 1871 census tells us that he was born in Ireland in 1835/36. It also records that he had a wife, Emma, 29, whose mother Elizabeth Ashton, a widow of 70, was living with them in Seacombe, now part of Wallasey. Mother and daughter were both born in Pilsworth, near Bury. The only possible record of a marriage found so far raises more questions than it answers. It took place at St Michael's in the Hamlet, Aigburth, on 29 August 1881 between Charles John Waldron, aged 48, a painter and bachelor of Solway Street, and Emma Ashton, a spinster aged 34, living in Lydia Street. Their names and his profession are correct, but the ages do not tally very closely with the censuses. Moreover, why are they listed as living in Toxteth when they had lived on the Wirral for more than a decade and continued to do so for the rest of their lives, and why would they have only married in 1881? If it is a different Charles and Emma Waldron, it is a remarkable coincidence of names and occupations. It is perhaps unresolvable at this distance in time.

Waldron was a member of the Liberal Party and served on the Wallasey Local Board from 1884 and was chairman of the health committee from 1886. He also stood for election to the Seacombe School Board as one of the nominated Roman Catholic members in 1889.[2]

Emma died aged 42 in January 1887, and in late 1889 Waldron married Ellen, the daughter of Job Luce, a publican. They were living at 78 Wheatland Lane, Poulton-cum-Seacombe, in 1891. He is listed as a 55-year-old retired painter and she is 24. They had a son, Frederick, aged 7 months. Waldron died later that year on 18 June 1891.

Ellen is listed as a widow in the census for 1901, 'living on her own means' in Great Crosby. Frederick was 10, and also listed is Dorothy Catherine, a daughter aged 3, who was born in St Asaph, North Wales. It is unclear who her father was.

Nothing is known about Waldron's artistic career and the only information comes from the dozen or so surviving paintings themselves. Signed examples date from the 1870s and 1880s. Virtually all of them were completed for American clients and are now in the United States.[3] Like Desilva (q.v.), it is likely that Waldron offered painted portraits to visiting captains who were purchasing paint and other related supplies for maintenance purposes during their stay in Liverpool. Waldron generally places the vessel in a port profile in the middle of the canvas, often in heavy seas,

Charles Waldron, *Phineas Pendleton*, signed and dated 1869, 77 x 123 cm. This canvas is typical of the portraits that Waldron produced, mainly of American vessels visiting Liverpool. (Penobscot Marine Museum)

---

1   *Liverpool Daily Post*, 2 December 1862.

2   *Birkenhead News*, 21 February 1885; *Liverpool Mercury*, 9 April 1884; *Birkenhead News*, 20 March 1887; *Liverpool Mercury*, 23 September 1889.

3   A painting of the Spanish SS *Leon XIII*, signed and dated 1884, was sold in Barcelona in 2015 and 2016.

with the minimum of other shipping. The background generally features a landmark, and the Fastnet Rock and South Stack lighthouses seem to have been particular favourites. His handling of the sea is accomplished but he sometimes has difficulty with perspective, as in the depiction of a distant schooner in *Phineas Pendleton*, which appears to hang above the sea near the horizon.

Lit.: Davidson 1986: 84, 89; Davidson 1995: 67.

Edward D. Walker (1937–2017)

Ted Walker was a professional marine artist for over fifty years and is known for his paintings and prints of a wide range historical subjects, including famous liners of the past such as *Titanic*, as well as contemporary subjects such as images of the famous Tall Ships Races.

Edward Donald Walker was born in Hull on 2 August 1937 to Albert and Isabella Walker. His father worked as a prison officer, and he had originally come from Hartlepool where the family had maritime connections. They moved to Merseyside after the Second World War. He married Susan Williamson in Crosby in 1971 and died on 11 April 2017, aged 80.

During his career, Walker produced many oil paintings, most of which were also made available as commercial and limited edition prints. His subjects ranged from Columbus's flagship *Santa Maria* to yachts off the Welsh coast, and included other famous ships such as the *Royal Charter*, Shackleton's *Endeavour* and the Merseyside-built Confederate ships *Alabama*, *Florida* and *Shenandoah*. Many of his paintings are set on the Mersey and he also painted various Mersey ferries, pilot boats and the Bar Lightship. One of his best-known works was a view of the *QE2* arriving in Liverpool on the occasion of her 25th anniversary in 1994. He also produced a series of paintings of *Titanic* and was the official artist to the RMS Titanic Artefacts Exhibitions.

Walker's painting of *Queen Mary 2* appeared on one of the Ocean Liners series of stamps in 2004, and in 2014 he was commissioned to produce artwork for two further stamps featuring the bulk carrier *Lord Hinton* and the Cunard paddle steamer *Britannia* (1840).

Two volumes of his paintings have appeared, *Sea Liverpool* (2006) and *Titanic* (2012), and an exhibition was held at WmAG in April 2012.

Lit.: Tibbles 1999: 198.

Ted Walker, *Lively Lady Rounding the Horn*, signed, 52 x 76 cm. In addition to his historical subjects, Walker painted contemporary events such as Alec Rose's single-handed voyage around the world in 1967. (ART UK/NML/MMM)

G. S. Walters, *Fishing Boats off Gorleston, East Anglia*, signed, 38 x 55 cm. Walters produced many similar atmospheric coastal views with shipping, usually featuring small local vessels. (Touchstone Rochdale, Rochdale Arts and Heritage Service)

George Stanfield Walters (1837–1924)

George Stanfield Walters was the eldest son of Samuel Walters (q.v.), and became a noted landscape and marine artist in his own right. Although he was born and brought up in Liverpool and lived there for a number of years, he relocated to London in his late twenties and was to remain there for the rest of his life.

Walters, whose middle name was given in tribute to the artist Clarkson Stanfield, was born in Liverpool in late 1837. He was educated at Liverpool Grammar School and then worked in his father's studio before joining the Liverpool Academy as a probationer in 1855 and as a student in the life school in 1856. He began exhibiting there from the age of 16.

Walters married Margaret Amelia Birrell at Christ Church, Newark-on-Trent, on 1 November 1864.[1] They moved to London shortly afterwards, where their sons, Ernest and Harold, were born in 1869 and 1872 respectively. Walters studied with Edward Duncan (1803–82), an old friend of his father's. The family was living at 11 Queen's Crescent in St Pancras in 1871. Margaret, known in the family as Meme, died on 17 April 1872, probably as a result of childbirth, and was buried in Highgate Cemetery. Two years later on 10 June 1874 Walters married Ann, the daughter of James Harris senior (1810–87), the well-known Swansea marine artist, in the parish church at Oystermouth. They were living at 134 Adelaide Road, Hampstead, in 1881 and 1891, but by 1901 they had moved to nearby 22 Maitland Park Villas, where they remained for the rest of their lives. They were sufficiently well-off to employ a general servant, and in 1881 also a nurse, and in 1891 a cook.

Walters died on 12 July 1924 and was buried alongside his first wife in Highgate Cemetery. Probate, in the sum of £450, was granted to his sons, Harold and Arthur, both chartered accountants.

Walters was a career artist and was an Associate of the Liverpool Academy (1861) and a member of the Royal Society of British Artists, Birmingham (1867). He exhibited frequently during his lifetime – at the RA 19 times, 1860–1915; Royal Society of British Artists, six times; Dudley and New Dudley Galleries, 17 times; Grosvenor Gallery, twice; Liverpool Walker Autumn Exhibitions, 19 times; Manchester, 12 times; Royal British Artists, 408 times; Royal Institute of Painters in Watercolours, 74 times; Royal Institute of Oil Painters, 48 times; the Royal Scottish Society of Painters in Watercolours, once; and 24 watercolours at Boston in 1896.

His marine works, in both oil and watercolour, are generally coastal and estuarine scenes featuring a range of small local and fishing craft. They are cleverly composed, usually peaceful, and often very atmospheric, with accurately portrayed vessels. One critic wrote that his work 'was characterised by delicacy and a beautiful finish'.[2] He also did some limited work for shipping companies, including producing postcards for Cunard.

There are examples of his oils in WmAG, WAG, Southampton City Art Gallery and of his watercolours in WAG, British Museum and Victoria and Albert Museum.

Lit.: Bennett 1978: 209; Davidson 1986: 138; Davidson 1992: 47–50; Morris and Roberts 1998: 622–23; Wright et al. 2006: 797.

---

1   His wife's name was Birrell, not Vinnell as stated by Davidson 1992: 47, and others.

2   Alfred Trumball, *Collector*, November 1896, quoted by Davidson 1992: 48–49.

Miles Walters (1772/73–1855)

Miles Walters was originally a ship's carpenter from Devon who spent thirteen years at sea before settling in London. He initially worked as a carpenter, but then began specialising in carving and gilding picture frames, and he also began to paint ship portraits. After a few years he moved first to Bristol and then settled permanently in Liverpool in about 1827. Shortly afterwards his son Samuel (q.v.) began assisting him and, since Samuel proved to be a more talented artist, his father gave up painting in about 1832. He went back to his original trade and concentrated on framing and related work. He maintained a successful carving and gilding business until he retired in about 1848.

Miles Walters was born in 1772/73, the son of John Walters (1748–c. 1826), a builder, carpenter and part-time artist, and his wife Mary.[1] He was baptised on 22 May 1774 in the parish church in Ilfracombe, Devon. A label on the back of one of his paintings tells us that 'the artist in his youthful days worked in a Mould Loft and has been thirteen years at sea'.[2] In fact, after completing his apprenticeship, he joined the Royal Navy. In 1797 when serving on HMS *Proselyte*, he made a will, naming his father John as his beneficiary.[3] A further reference in the register of allotments in 1799 confirms that he was a member of the carpenter's crew on HMS *Proselyte*.[4]

Walters seems to have left the sea around 1806, and on 4 November the following year he married Maria Groves at Westbury-on-Trym, on the outskirts of Bristol. They were living in London when their eldest daughter Elizabeth was born in November 1809, and Samuel was born there two years later. The children were not baptised until September 1813, when the family was living in Willow Street, Shoreditch, and Walters gave his occupation as carpenter. He was again listed as a carpenter of Willow Street when his youngest son, John, was baptised in January 1814.

Although there is no definite information, Walters probably began specialising in picture frames and undertaking ship portraits in about 1820. The London directories list him as a 'carver and gilder' at Edward Street, Limehouse Fields, from 1823, and his earliest surviving paintings, all of London-registered vessels, although unsigned, probably date from the early 1820s. The label previously referred to, probably dating from about 1825 and including the Limehouse address, also includes the statement that the artist 'has painted upwards of two hundred ships in the past six years'.

Despite this successful level of activity, at some time around 1826 Walters clearly decided to try his fortune away from London. A group of nearly a dozen paintings with Bristol-based subjects can be dated to around 1826–27, which suggests that he was based in the city at this time. He probably moved to Liverpool in 1827 when he completed the portrait of *John Taylor* (signed and dated 1827), and he was listed under artists (marine) in *Pigot's Directory* at 17 Pleasant Street, Liverpool, in 1828. He was living in Harford Street, Toxteth, and his occupation given as artist, when his sons John Groves and William Miles were baptised as teenagers at St Andrew's Church on 27 March 1829.

Around the time of the move to Liverpool, his eldest son, Samuel, who was about 16, began assisting his father, and the majority of paintings from 1828 onwards are signed 'Walters and Son'. Initially the hand of the younger man is hard to detect, but by the early 1830s his influence is clear. Both father and son entered paintings separately for the Liverpool Academy exhibition in 1831 and again in 1832. Samuel's earliest independent painting dates from 1831 and it seems that the elder Walters, recognising his son's greater talent, gave up painting ship portraits and concentrated on the carving and gilding trade. The end of their joint arrangement was officially confirmed in 1838 when 'Miles Walters and Samuel Walters, Liverpool, marine painters, carvers and gilders' dissolved their partnership.[5] When his two youngest sons, William Miles and John Groves, held joint weddings in April 1840 at St Philip's Church,

---

1   If he was 82 in August 1855, he would have been born between August 1772 and July 1773.

2   On the back of a portrait of *Commerce*, showing an incident between 1820 and 1825; Davidson 1992: 19.

3   TNA, ADM/48/100.

4   TNA, ADM/27/5.

5   *The Globe*, 7 July 1838.

Miles Walters, *Ship William Miles of Bristol*, signed and dated 1825, 47 x 79 cm. Like the majority of Walters' Bristol pictures, this portrait of the *William Miles* in two views is set off the island of Flatholm in the Bristol Channel. (© Bristol Museums, Galleries & Archives, Purchased 1936/Bridgeman Images)

Miles Walters, *Antigua Packet*, 47 x 79 cm. This view of the *Antigua Packet* is an example of a group of paintings set off Egremont, on the Wirral coast. (NML/MMM)

Miles was listed as a carver and gilder. He had moved to premises at 3 Berry Street, and he was living there with his wife and daughter in 1841. They were employing a female servant, which suggests that the business was proving successful.

His wife Maria died from asthma on 10 July 1847, and though the death occurred at Egremont on the Wirral, Walters was still based at Berry Street. Shortly afterwards in 1848, when he was in his mid-seventies, he gave up business, and his son William, who had been working with his father for many years, took over.

It is not entirely clear where Walters spent his last years. He is almost certainly the Miles Walters who at the time of the 1851 census was living at 6 York Terrace in Stepney, close to where he had lived and worked more than thirty years earlier. Although he is listed as a 65-year-old widower when he was in fact 78, and his birthplace is given as South Molton, Devon, rather than Ilfracombe, which is about twenty miles away, no other Miles Walters has been traced. His status as 'independent' would be compatible with being retired and financially secure. He was definitely living in Stepney on 28 October 1851 when he married Maria Tyler, a widow, at St Leonard's Church, Shoreditch. He was described as a widower and 'marine artist', the son of John Walters, a builder, which confirms the identification.[1] There is no way of knowing how the marriage came about and whether he had previously known her.

Walters had returned to Liverpool by 1855 and was living at 5 Mile Street, Toxteth, when he died on 7 August. His occupation is given as 'formerly a marine painter – master', suggesting perhaps that he and his family regarded his legacy as an artist rather than a tradesman. He was buried in the Necropolis, later known as Low Hill Cemetery.

Miles Walters had a very distinctive style, very much akin to the vernacular art of the period, typified by the work of his father, John. Although naive in appearance with rather stylised seas, the vessels themselves are very faithfully depicted and his training as a seafarer and ship's carpenter comes out in his careful and accurate representation of the rigging, deck gear and other details. His portraits are always of specific, identifiable vessels and make good use of flag codes and name pennants. His canvases are significantly wider than high, allowing him to show the vessel in two or three views, and they include a variety of other shipping and small local craft which makes for most interesting and attractive compositions. The scenes are set in specific locations – all his London pictures are set off Dover and the vast majority of his Bristol pictures are set off Flatholm in the Bristol Channel. For his Liverpool paintings the most frequent location is in the Mersey off Egremont, at the northern end of the Wirral, with a small number set off the Perch Rock fort, and another group off the Liverpool side of the river with Everton in the background. Another popular location is off the South Stack lighthouse, Anglesey, on the approach to the Mersey. All the backgrounds are painted in considerable detail and add significantly to the overall appearance of his paintings.

The overwhelming majority of the paintings dating from his Liverpool period are signed 'Walters and Son', but the composition and most of the execution appears to be by Miles or certainly in his distinctive style. The paintings from about 1830 onwards show the hand of Samuel coming through with increasing confidence, usually in the detailed handling of such elements as the sails or the depiction of the master or crew on board, which are shown with a realism lacking in the father's early paintings. Davidson's biography of Samuel Walters illustrates virtually all the works attributed to Miles Walters and Walters and Son.

Walters is only represented in public collections in the UK by a handful of works, the largest number being at MMM, with single works in NMM, Hull and Bristol, and in the US in PEM and MM. A significant number of works are in private collections, mainly in the UK and US.

---

1 She was born on 19 July 1797, the daughter of Thomas Dunn, a butcher, and his wife Anna, of Holywell Street, Shoreditch, and was baptised at St Leonard's, Shoreditch, on 22 August. She married William Henry Tyler at Christ Church, Spitalfields, on 25 November 1827.

Lit.: Davidson 1992; Davidson 1995: 17; Finamore 1995: 43–45; Morris and Roberts 1998: 623; Tibbles 1999: 200–03; Wright et al. 2006: 797.

Miles and Samuel Walters, *Arab*, signed, 59 x 87 cm. Whilst the overall composition follows that employed by Miles Walters, the influence of his son can be seen in the more naturalistic treatment of the sea and some of the detail. (ARTUK/NML/MMM)

Samuel Walters (1811–1882)

Samuel Walters was probably the most successful and talented ship portraitist to work in Liverpool in the nineteenth century. He began his artistic career assisting his father, Miles Walters (q.v.), but soon established himself as an important painter in his own right. He was an inventive and commercially minded artist, not only producing a range of ship portraits in oils but arranging for many of his paintings to be engraved, and in his later years he showed an interest in photography and sold photographic prints and pocket-sized *cartes-de-visite* of his paintings. In addition to more than 300 surviving ship portraits, he also produced a significant number of more general marine scenes.

Walters was born on 1 November 1811 in Spitalfields, London, the son of Miles Walters and his wife Maria. He was baptised, along with his elder sister Elizabeth, at St Leonard's Church, Shoreditch, on 26 September 1813. Nothing is known of his childhood, but the family moved to Bristol in about 1826 and then settled in Liverpool in 1827. By this time, Walters had begun assisting his father in producing ship portraits, the earliest examples of their joint work being two paintings, the *P.S. Glamorgan off the Coast* and the *P.S. Palmerston Entering Hotwell Dock, Bristol*, both signed and dated 'Walters and Son 1827'. At this stage the younger man's input is hard to identify, but over the next five years his role and influenced increased, to the extent that his father relinquished his role as a painter himself and concentrated on the subsidiary business of carving and gilding and producing frames.[1]

Walters initially studied at the Liverpool Mechanical School of Arts and exhibited his first work, *Dutch Boats in a Breeze*, at the Liverpool Academy in 1830. In December that year he was admitted as a probationer at the Academy, and in 1831 joined the drawing classes under the tutelage of Alexander Mosses (1793–1837), where he remained until 1835. Even before he had completed his studies, he was taking commissions. He is listed as a marine artist in the local directories from 1834, working from his father's shop at 28 Berry Street.

On 16 September 1835 he married Betsey Staniland Pilley, the daughter of Michael Pilley, a cloth dealer, from Thorne, Yorkshire. The ceremony took place in Selby Abbey, close to the bride's home. Their first son, Henry, was born in Nelson Street, Liverpool, in August 1836, and they went on to have eight more children over the next twenty years.

Although only in his mid-twenties, Walters was already making a name for himself and showing the business acumen for which he was known throughout his career. One of his earliest works was a painting of a great storm that hit Liverpool and the north-west of England in December 1833. In 1836 he arranged for this to be reproduced as an engraving under the title *Port of Liverpool*, attracting the attention of the local press for his 'most spirited representation' of the event.[2] It is perhaps not surprising that he was elected as an Associate of the Liverpool Academy in 1837.

Whilst his career burgeoned, all was not plain sailing on the personal front. In December 1839 his eldest son Henry and his young daughter Ann Maria caught scarlet fever and died. Only a few months later, in February 1840, the Great George's Congregational Chapel, where the family worshipped, burned down. Walters produced a painting of the event, in which he included members of his family in the crowd watching the conflagration. He sold prints of the painting for the rebuilding fund.

In these early years Walters spent some time travelling, visiting amongst other places the Thames and Medway, Scarborough, Hastings, Plymouth and the Netherlands. When the census was taken in 1841, he was staying at the Stafford Arms in Pimlico. Betsey and their two surviving children, George Stansfield, aged 3, and Robert, aged 9 months, were at home in Nelson Street. He was clearly successful enough to be employing two young sisters as domestic servants.

By 1844 they had moved to Stanhope Terrace on the north-eastern edge of the town. However, the following year, Walters made the decision to move to London.

---

1   It seems that they had had a formal relationship, as a list of partnerships dissolved in 1838 includes 'Miles Walters and Samuel Walters, Liverpool, marine painters, and carvers and gilders'; *Globe*, 7 July 1838.

2   *Liverpool Mail*, 15 September 1836.

He resigned from the Liverpool Academy on 12 August, and in October an announcement appeared in the press that an auction of 'Modern Furniture, Valuable paintings etc.' would take place on the 'instructions of Mr Samuel Walters, who is leaving Liverpool'.[1] Taken together, these two events suggest that the move was intended to be more than temporary. The reasons for the relocation are not clear, but it has been suggested that the death in May 1845 of William Huggins (1781–1845), one of the foremost marine painters, opened up an opportunity for a new marine artist to take his place in the capital. In fact, Walters was able to base himself at Huggins's old studio at 105 Leadenhall Street, from where Huggins's son-in-law, Edward Duncan (1803–85), a noted engraver of marine prints whom Walters might have already known, also operated. Walters and his family went to live three miles away at 16 Trafalgar Terrace, Mortimer Road, West Hackney, where their daughter, Maria Groves, was born on 20 September 1846.

Whether the opportunities offered in the capital did not materialise in the way he had anticipated, or whether they perhaps missed other members of the close-knit family, Walters and his family were back in Liverpool by mid-1847, living not far from their previous home at 56 Upper Stanhope Street. He re-established his studio at the Berry Street premises of his father and his brother, William Miles, who took over the operation of the carving and gilding business in 1848. By the time the census was taken in 1851, he was still living there and the family had expanded to four sons and two daughters, ranging in age from 2 to 13. They continued to employ a young female servant.

Walters was getting good commissions and received regular publicity for his paintings. For instance, his portrait of SS *Great Britain*, recently completed for the owners, Gibbs, Bright & Co., was placed on view to the public at his brother's premises, by then located in the more fashionable Bold Street, in 1852.[2] Similarly his painting of the yacht *Coralie*, which had won the Queen's Cup at the Royal Mersey Regatta in 1853, and a painting of the *Lightning off the Great Orme* were displayed in the Exchange Rooms in 1854.[3] He supplied paintings for many of the leading shipping companies of the period, including Cunard, Inman, Brocklebank, Bibby and Elder Dempster, and for local shipbuilders such as Thomas Royden. He was also popular with American owners, including the owners of the ill-fated Collins Line.

Throughout these years, Walters exhibited up to half a dozen works virtually every year at the Liverpool Academy. For a few years, from 1859 to 1862, he showed his work at the rival Liverpool Society of Fine Arts and served a term on the council of the Society in 1860.[4] He also exhibited a painting on a fairly regular basis at the RA, from 1842 until 1861, and again at the Liverpool Academy exhibitions and at the Suffolk Street Gallery, London, in the 1870s. Additionally, he showed his work at the Royal Art Institution in Dublin, where he won two prizes of £15 and £6 in 1848.[5]

In 1855 Walters, perhaps beginning to enjoy the fruits of his success, moved out of Liverpool to Falkner Terrace, Bootle, on the northern edge of the dock estate, which had excellent views of the Mersey. This was his recorded residence in the 1861 census, by which time his eldest sons were making their way in the world. George Stansfield, now 23, was listed as a landscape artist, Robert, 20, was a corn merchant's apprentice and Samuel, 18, had left home to begin a seafaring career.

Walters is known to have been interested in photography, and this began to have some influence on his work. When he was asked to undertake a painting for the Royal National Lifeboat Institution showing a rescue off the east coast, 'he was induced to prepare it, at considerable trouble, by a peculiar process of photography, in order to bring before the public a correct and picturesque view of one of these lifeboats'.[6] In the following two decades he photographed a number of his paintings and sold photographic prints of them, some of

1   *Liverpool Mercury*, 24 October 1845.
2   *Liverpool Mercury*, 13 April 1852.
3   *Liverpool Mail*, 6 May 1854.
4   *Liverpool Daily Post*, 12 March 1860.
5   *The Pilot*, 3 April 1848.
6   *Illustrated London News*, 7 April 1860.

Samuel Walters, *P S Ethiope off the Coast of West Africa*, 58 x 92 cm. This painting probably dates from 1840–45 when the vessel was employed in exploring the rivers of the Niger delta with a view to establish trading links with the interior. (NML/MMM)

Samuel Walters, *Irlam Pilot Sloop No.6*, signed and dated 1834, 69 x 98 cm. This detailed portrait of a pilot vessel is typical of Walters' early work. (NML/MMM)

which were hand-coloured in oils. He also produced a series of miniature photographs printed on cards measuring 10 cm by 4 cm, describing himself as 'S Walters / Publisher of Marine Photographs'. They were almost exclusively of transatlantic steamships and many carry an accommodation plan on the reverse, indicating perhaps that they were primarily intended as souvenirs for the passengers.

By 1871 all the children had left home, and when the census was taken Walters seems to have been on one of his trips away, as he and Betsey are listed as visitors in the home of Josiah Williams, a seed and corn merchant, in Beaumaris on Anglesey. It is perhaps not surprising that such a base, close to many of the locations used in his paintings, would appeal to him.

Now in his sixties, although still active and highly regarded, Walters seems to have taken life somewhat easier and there are fewer paintings dating from the last decade or so or his life. In the mid-1870s further dock development had begun to encroach along the Bootle shoreline, and Walters purchased a plot of land slightly further inland where he built two houses at 76 and 78 Merton Road. He moved into number 76 in 1877 and was living there with Betsey and a female servant at the time of the census in 1881. A visitor from Yorkshire, Mary Gutteridge, a widow and perhaps an old friend of Betsey's, was staying with them.

Samuel Walters died from cancer on 5 March 1882, aged 70, and was buried in Anfield Cemetery. His death not only saw obituaries in the local press but in the *Pall Mall Gazette* and the *Illustrated London News*.[1] An auction of his studio, which included about 200 of his works and some paintings by other artists he had acquired, was held on 5 June 1882.[2] He left nearly £3,500, a substantial sum. His widow continued to live at Merton Road but later moved to Birkdale, where she died, aged 79, in 1891. She was buried in Anfield Cemetery with her husband.

Walters was a prolific artist whose career spanned more than fifty years. He began by assisting his father

when he was 16, and more than thirty surviving paintings are signed or attributed to Walters and Son. Initially both the composition and execution followed the naive style set by his father, but over the next four or five years Walters made his influence felt, and the depiction of the vessels, the seas and other detail become increasingly naturalistic. When he began painting on his own, although certain elements of his father's style remained, as in the rather mechanical handling of the sea in the portraits of *Andromeda* (Hull Museums) or *Higginson* (National Museum of American History), he soon demonstrated his own characteristic style, as in the *Zephyr* of 1832 (MMM). Many of the paintings from the mid-1830s show a youthful exuberance, with bright skies and banks of cloud, and lots of activity on the water in addition to the main subject, and though the seas often appear rather sculpted, there is frequently a clever interplay of light, with areas of creamy hollows contrasting with the bluey-green waves. A typical example is the Liverpool pilot boat *Irlam* of 1834 (MMM) or the *Euphrates* (NMM) shown off Cape Town in two views, with other vessels and a small fishing boat and its crew highlighted in the foreground.

Many of his paintings completed in the 1830s and 1840s continue to show a similarly imaginative approach, immediately appealing to the eye and providing lots of interest for the enquiring mind, working out the movement of the vessel or finding the story of what is happening. This is illustrated by some of his paintings commemorating a specific event, such as his series of four paintings of the *Burning of the Ocean Monarch* in 1846 or his *Bon Voyage to Jenny Lind* of 1850 (PEM), which are masterly depictions, full of interest and beautifully painted.

However, by the mid-1850s subtle changes were beginning to happen. Walters adopts a greater fluidity, with a looser approach to the depiction of the sea, which often becomes flatter with more elongated waves. More vessels are depicted at sea or with less detailed backgrounds and the overall atmosphere is rather more monochrome. His portrayal of the pilot boat *The Duke* of 1854 (MMM) contrasts interestingly with the *Irlam* of twenty years earlier. The sea is flatter and more monotonous, and whilst the boat itself is more forward

---

1   *Liverpool Mercury*, 8 March 1882; *Pall Mall Gazette*, 9 March 1882; *Illustrated London News*, 25 March 1882.
2   *Liverpool Mercury*, 26 May 1882.

Samuel Walters, *P S Banshee*, signed and dated 1864, 50 x 80 cm. This portrait of the Confederate paddle steamer *Banshee* typifies Walters in his later years. Although an accurate portrait of the vessel, it lacks flair and does not contain any of the detail that helps enliven many of his youthful and mature paintings. (NML/MMM)

Samuel Walters, *Euphrates off Table Mountain*, signed and dated 1835, 97 x 153 cm. This large and action-packed canvas shows Walters' youthful exuberance, with its clever use of light both in the sky and the highlights of the sea. (National Maritime Museum, Greenwich, London)

on the canvas, it adopts a less interesting pose and other detail is relegated to the far distance. The excitement and interplay of the various elements has gone.

By the 1860s and 1870s, although Walters continued to produce finely crafted and satisfying portraits, he is more likely to adopt a standard profile and he tends to use a duller, greyish or yellow-brown palette. Increasingly, his subjects are steamships, and although still requiring considerable amounts of sail at times, the opportunities for creating interesting and exciting portraits were probably more limited than with the vagaries of sailing vessels. Three paintings in MMM, *Domitila*, 1863, *Morocco*, 1862, and *PS Banshee*, 1864, are typical of his later works. He still produced striking images – his *City of Brussels* (WAG) of about 1869, showing the steamer battling valiantly against heavy seas, the sky riven between dark and foreboding rain-laden clouds and the golden glow of a setting sun, is a thrilling composition. He also produced a wonderfully evocative and highly detailed panorama of the Liverpool waterfront in his *Port of Liverpool* of 1873 (WAG), which must surely be one of his most iconic paintings. It was reproduced as an engraving in 1877, and photographic prints of the painting were also available.

His earliest exhibited work was a painting of Dutch vessels in a breeze, and throughout his career he produced similar, more generic marine views. He seems to have particularly favoured this type of subject for showing at the academic exhibitions in both Liverpool and London. They clearly appealed to a different market to his ship portraits, but might, perhaps, have given him greater satisfaction, as many of them remained in his ownership and were passed on to members of the family.

Walters's ship portraiture is richly represented in British and American collections, particularly in the MMM, NMM, MM and PEM. There are many paintings in private collections and they appear regularly on the market.

An exhibition of his work, including 48 oils, 5 watercolours and 20 prints, was held at the Bootle Art Gallery from 6 April to 2 May 1959. Descendants of the artist loaned ten paintings of his more general marine subjects.

Lit.: Anonymous 1959; Davidson 1992; Davidson 1995: 18; Finamore 1995: 46, 48, 51, 53, 56, 58; Morris and Roberts 1998: 623–24; Tibbles 1999: 201–33; Wright et al. 2006: 797.

Samuel Walters, *The Departure of Miss Jenny Lind in the U.S. Mail Steam Ship Atlantic, 1850*, 90 x 146 cm. This is one of Walters' most accomplished canvases, with a myriad of activity depicted and executed with skill and bravura. (Courtesy of the Peabody Essex Museum)

Richard Wane, *The Lonely Watch*, signed, 67 x 127 cm. This picture was purchased for the Walker Art Gallery's collection at the Liverpool Autumn Exhibition in 1904. (ARTUK/NML/WAG)

Richard Wane (1852–1904)

Richard Whittaker Wane was a landscape and marine artist who was highly regarded in his own lifetime and exhibited regularly at all the major exhibitions in London and elsewhere. He lived in a number of places before settling on the Wirral in 1896, where he remained until his death.

Wane was born on 3 April 1852 in Manchester, the son of William Wane. Details of his childhood have not been traced, but by 1871 he was living with his elder brother, Marshall, a photographer, and his young family

in Douglas on the Isle of Man. He was already describing his occupation as 'artist'. Despite his Manchester birth, the *Isle of Man Times* claimed him as a Manx artist into the 1890s, and on one occasion commented on his 'having been bred here', which suggests that he might have spent some of his formative years on the island.[1] Although he married Marian Millinger, the daughter

---

1 *Isle of Man Times*, 25 May 1895. He has not been traced in the 1861 census, but was not living with his brother, who was resident in Douglas according to the census.

of a mariner, in Everton in December 1871, their first child, Ethel, was born at 2 Sydney Street, Douglas, on 15 October 1872. Their daughter Maud was also born there in 1874.

They were living back in Manchester at 58 Talbot Street, Moss Side, in October 1879 when their son Harold was born, and were still there when the census was taken in 1881. Wane describes himself as 'painter landscape'. He seems to have made regular trips back to the Isle of Man and was sketching there in the summer of 1879. It was also around this time that he began to expand his work to include 'sea pieces'.[1]

During the 1880s Wane's career took off and he moved location frequently – he was in Conway in 1883, Deganwy in 1887, Llandudno in 1889, and by 1890 the family was living in Dulwich, South London, where their youngest daughter, Dorothy, was born. His wife and the five children were living at 106 East Dulwich Grove in 1891, but Wane himself was not present. The house was called appropriately 'Min-y-don', which means 'sound of the sea' in Welsh. He was still resident there in 1893.[2] In 1896 they moved to Egremont, between Wallasey and New Brighton, where they were living with their five children, all unmarried, at 13 Kingslake Road in 1901. Wane initially had a studio at 100 Victoria Road, New Brighton, but by 1899 he was sharing a studio with E. C. Quayle (1872–1946) at Canning Chambers in South John Street.

Wane was a member of the Dudley Art Gallery Society, London, the Royal Society of British Artists and the Liverpool Sketching Club, of which he was, for a time, president. He exhibited at the RA, the Royal Institution of Oil Painters, the New Watercolour Society, the Royal Hibernian Academy, the Royal Scottish Academy, the Royal Cambrian Society and the Liverpool Autumn Exhibitions. His paintings were frequently mentioned in press reviews of the various exhibitions with approval – his 'seascapes are, as usual, vigorous and dashing and full of daylight. He is rapidly becoming one of our most able exponents of the breezy atmosphere of coastal scenes.'[3] A number of newspapers reporting on the RA Summer Exhibition of 1889 drew attention to 'a magnificent seascape, the work of Mr Richard Wane, of whom Sir Frederick Leighton [president of the Academy] has said some encouraging things'.[4]

Wane suffered from ill-health in his later years, and died at home at 57 Church Street, Poulton-cum-Seacombe, on 8 January 1904, leaving effects worth £403 to his widow.

Wane's marine paintings are mostly coastal views, often with a small boat or a few figures in the foreground, but sometimes just natural scenes of the sea and the coastal features. Some of his paintings also feature fishing vessels as the main subject, such as the lively *Oyster Catching* in WmAG. His paintings are mostly set off familiar landmarks and coastal scenes, the most popular locations being off the Isle of Man and North Wales, but also around the Mersey and off the Scottish coast. He worked in both oil and watercolour. He is best represented in the collections of WmAG, but there are typical works in WAG, with Manx Heritage, and in a number of provincial galleries.

Lit.: Bennett 1978: 214; Wright et al. 2006: 799.

---

1   *Isle of Man Times*, 6 March 1880.
2   Electoral Roll, Southwark, 1893.
3   *Isle of Man Times*, 13 February 1886, quoting a review in the *Manchester Evening Mail*.
4   *Nottingham Evening Post*, 1 May 1889.

Richard Wareing (1832/33–1912)

Only a handful of signed paintings by Wareing are currently known, but another group of unsigned paintings which are very similar and were initially attributed to an unknown artist given the pseudonym 'Gothic Scroll' might also be by him. The paintings not only share stylistic characteristics but also compositional features and their unusually long width and narrow height. There is some further confusion because of the spelling of his name, which is usually given as 'Wareing' but occasionally as 'Waring'.

Although his marriage certificates tell us that his father was Thomas Wareing, a silversmith, his origins and early life cannot be traced. From later information we know that he was born in Liverpool, probably about 1832/33. The earliest documented reference dates from March 1854, when as an 18-year-old Wareing left Birkenhead on the *Jenny Jones* for a voyage to Dundalk. There is one other reference to his seafaring career, from the crew lists, which shows that he was due to sail on SS *Greece* of Liverpool as an able seaman in January 1874, earning £4.10.0 per week, but he failed to join the vessel as expected.

Wareing married Ellen Calvert, the daughter of a bookkeeper, at St Peter's, Liverpool, on 18 January 1858, when he was described as a mariner of College Lane. They were lodging with a blacksmith off Scotland Road in 1861, when he was described as a mariner and Ellen listed as a milliner. In 1871 they were living at 84 Benledi Road, and his occupation was confirmed as a mariner. Ellen died at some point after this, and on 14 August 1877 Wareing married widow Ann Maria Jamieson (née Mounsey) at St Peter's, Liverpool. In the census in 1881 he is listed as a 46-year-old Liverpool-born mariner living in Lower Grove Street, Everton, with his wife, a step-daughter Margaret, and a lodger and young visitor.

Wareing probably left the sea sometime during the following decade, and is listed in *Gore's Directory* for 1889 under the name Richard Wareing as a marine artist, living at 41 Rockley Street, Kirkdale. In the 1891 census he is shown at the same address under the name Richard Waring, living with his wife Ann and step-granddaughter. His occupation is given as a marine artist. His wife died in 1898, and in 1901 he was living in Netherfield Road, Kirkdale, with his sister-in-law, Mary Geron, who was acting as his housekeeper. He is described as an artist painter living by his 'own account' and working 'at home'.

Ten years later in 1911 he was a resident of the Liverpool Home of Aged Mariners, based in Liscard, when he was described as a widower and retired mariner. His residence is confirmed by the signature on the 1912 painting of *Karina*: 'R. Waring / Mariners Home / Egremont / 1912'. He died there in the late summer of 1913, aged 80.

Wareing's paintings demonstrate a naive style which is particularly noticeable in the stick-like figures that inhabit the decks and the characteristic way of depicting many of the details of the vessel, including the rigging and the rails. The yards are shown parallel to the hull and the short black strokes indicating the ropes securing the furled sails are distinctive. The artist also has a characteristic way of portraying flags in a rather flat manner, but so that they are fully visible. Incidental detail, such as other shipping and buildings, is often portrayed out of scale to the main subject (a good example of this being the gig boat and tug in *SS City of Cambridge*, MMM).

A number of the unsigned paintings bear a distinctive scroll along the bottom of the picture, with Gothic-style lettering recording the name of the shipping line, the name of the vessel, the master and the tonnage. From this information they can be dated from the mid-1870s to the mid-1880s. Signed paintings bear dates from 1884 to 1912.

Although some paintings are on canvas, many of them, particularly those with the Gothic scroll, are on a thin oblong metal sheet which is generally about twice as wide as it is high. The metal of one of the paintings, *SS Sardinian* (MMM), has been analysed as white brass and it is assumed that the other metal sheets used are of a similar material.

Lit.: Davidson 1986: 138; Tibbles 1999: 148–52; Wright et al. 2006: 179.

The City Line Company's S.S. "City of Cambridge," of Glasgow, 1489 tons reg, W. Jack, Commander.

Richard Wareing, *City of Cambridge Entering the Mersey*, 44 x 84 cm. This portrait illustrates all the characteristics of this group of paintings by Wareing, with an inscription in Gothic lettering, the stick-like figures on deck and rigging with all sails furled. (ARTUK/NML/MMM)

Samuel Williamson (1792–1840)

Samuel Williamson was a landscape and marine painter whose main marine work featured local fishing boats and coastal scenes.

Williamson was born in Liverpool in about 1792, the son of portrait painter John Williamson (1751–1818), who had moved from Birmingham where he had initially worked as a decorator in a japanning works. Almost nothing has been found about Williamson's personal life, though he might have been the father of landscape artist Daniel Alexander Williamson. *Gore's Directory* shows that he was living at 15 Benson Street in 1825, when he was listed as 'artist', and he was at the same address in 1829. This appears to have been a family home as it was given as his father's address when he died in June 1818. Williamson was still living in Benson Street when he died on 7 June 1840.[1] An obelisk to his memory was erected in St James's Cemetery in 1842.

Williamson was an Associate of the Liverpool Academy when it was founded in 1810 and became a full member the following year. He exhibited regularly until 1831, when he resigned, and again after 1838 when he was re-elected. He was the subject of an artistic controversy in 1828 when his painting *North Shore, Liverpool* (WAG) won the Corporation's Prize of £20 for best oil painting, and divided local opinion between those favouring a classical style and those, like Williamson, representing a free approach, influenced by Turner. He also exhibited at the RA in 1811 and later in Manchester, Birmingham and Leeds. He is said to have travelled abroad, and a number of continental scenes painted by him survive.

Williamson's marine paintings generally feature fishing vessels and fishermen either on the shore or in coastal views, often with a local Merseyside background. These include views from Bootle Sands and Birkenhead, and a view of New Brighton. There are good examples in WmAG and WAG, which also has a number of drawings by him formerly in the collection of Joseph Mayer.

---

1 'On 7th inst., Mr. Samuel Williamson, Landscape-painter of Benson Street, Liverpool', *Manchester Courier and Lancashire General Advertiser*, 13 June 1840.

Lit.: Bennett 1978: 225–27; Davidson 1986: 139; *ODNB*; Lee 1900: 8–9; Morris and Roberts 1998: 656; Wright et al. 2006: 829.

Samuel Williamson, *Fishing Boat in Heavy Seas*, 67 x 135 cm. This action-packed view out at sea is in sharp contrast to Williamson's more tranquil coastal scenes. (ART UK/NML/WAG)

Joseph Witham (1832–1901)

Joseph Witham was active as a marine painter in Liverpool in the last quarter of the nineteenth century, generally producing fairly standard ship portraits. Before arriving in Liverpool, he spent a number of years as a bookseller in London and might have spent some time at sea.

Witham was the son of Joseph Witham, a cabinet maker, and his wife Sarah, and was born at South Berksted on the outskirts of Bognor Regis in Sussex, where he was baptised Isaac Joseph on 11 February 1832. He was living there in West Street in 1841 with his parents and younger sister, Mary.

According to an article in the *Liverpool Daily Post* of 16 November 1928 he worked as a seafarer and sailed from Liverpool for a number of years when he was young. This would explain why he was not listed in the censuses for 1851 and 1861. He married Sarah Saunders, the daughter of a cabinet proprietor, at All Souls Church in Marylebone, London, on 7 July 1857, and their son Frederick was born in St Pancras in early 1861. When his daughter Eve was baptised on 7 July 1867, he was living at 205 Grays Inn Road, and his occupation was given as bookseller. His son Walter was born in 1870 and in the census of the following year Witham and his family were at the same address, and he was described as 'bookseller and marine artist'.

The family had moved to Liverpool by 1874, when Witham first appears in the local directories as an artist living at 23 Seacombe Street. Perhaps he had decided to pursue his artistic career more vigorously, and Liverpool was the obvious choice, particularly if he already knew the town from his seafaring days. In later directories he is listed specifically as 'marine artist' and this is how he is described in the 1881 census, when he and his family were living at 27 Wentworth Road, Everton. By 1891 his children had all left home and he and Sarah were living at 117 Granton Road, Everton, and he was again listed as a marine artist. Sarah died in the autumn of 1897 at the age of 65. Witham was listed as a 69-year-old marine artist living as a boarder at 12 Church Place, Everton, in the 1901 census. His landlady was a 38-year-old widow who was living with her daughter, son and mother, and who was working as an office cleaner. According to a former member of the Cape Horners' Association, Mrs Amy Martin, who knew Witham at this time, he began to lose his eyesight in his later years and his output declined markedly. He died on 14 October 1901 at 25 Sever Street, Everton, from a 'growth of the gullet'.

There is some slight confusion over Witham's name. He seems to have generally been known only by the name Joseph, but his birth and death certificates record him as Isaac Joseph. Additionally, when he married and when his daughter was baptised he gave his name as Isaac Joseph Clark Witham.

Given the relatively small number of his known paintings, it seems unlikely that he was able to make a living purely as an artist, but apart from one entry in the 1892 directory when he is listed as a glass decorator, there is no indication of another occupation when he lived in Liverpool. He seems to have briefly formed some sort of partnership with the Walters family, and a painting of the steamship *Egypt* (Hull Museums) gives his address as 118 Bold Street, where William Walters, younger brother of Samuel Walters, ran the family picture-framing business. Furthermore, in 1878 a couple of advertisements appeared in the local press under the heading 'Marine paintings, J Witham & Wm M Walters, Marine Artists and Ship Portrait Painters'. On the first occasion they offered 'a fine painting of a Liverpool Pilot Boat on duty off the port' and on the second occasion 'a portrait of the New Royal Mail Steamship Spanish Reina Mercedes'. They also offered 'Portraits of Yachts and Ships from 5 guineas to 100 and upwards'.[1] The exact nature of the partnership and their respective responsibilities are not clear, but it looks as though Witham was producing the paintings and Walters was providing his services as a framer and dealer. The arrangement does not appear to have been particularly successful as there are no further references to it.

In Witham's portraits the subject generally fills the majority of the canvas, and is often shown with a rather sketchy background or other shipping indistinctly indicated near the horizon. The seas are often stormy

---

1   *Liverpool Mercury*, 9 May 1878, 9 August 1878.

Joseph Witham, *Graceful*, signed and dated 1894, 61 x 92 cm. This view of a coastal steamer uses the muted colours favoured by Witham. (ARTUK/NML/MMM)

and he seems to have been attracted to dramatic and colourful skies. His most impressive painting is probably of the *SS Sarmartian* (MMM), which shows the vessel about to the leave the Mersey on 14 November 1878 carrying Queen Victoria's daughter, the Princess Louise, and her husband the Marquess of Lorne on their way to take up his appointment as Governor-General of Canada. In keeping with such an occasion, the ship and the accompanying vessels, including one of the local steam tugs, are dressed with a variety of flags. A more detailed than usual view of the Wirral shore and the Perch Rock fort and lighthouse are also included. Another memorable canvas depicts an incident on 8 February 1881 when the No. 2 Liverpool pilot boat *Leader* led a group of twelve vessels over the bar at the entrance to the Mersey during a gale. Witham produced a number of versions of this subject with only slight variations of detail.

There are good examples of his work in MMM, NMM, NMW, Hull and Grimsby.

His second son, Walter (1870–after 1936), was a landscape artist whose known works include river, lake and mountain views, as well as country scenes of rural cottages, mainly in watercolour.

Lit.: Davidson 1986: 103–05, 111; Davidson 1995: 23; Finamore 1995: 73, 76; Tibbles 1999: 237–41; Wright et al. 2006: 838.

Richard Wright, *A Man of War in a Harbour*, c. 1765–70, 130 x 193 cm. Wright painted a number of similar canvases of unknown vessels in anonymous settings. (NML/WAG)

Richard Wright (probably 1723–c. 1775)

Richard Wright is the earliest maritime painter associated with Liverpool. He was probably born in the town and lived there until his late thirties, when he moved to London. Almost all his known work dates from the period after he left Liverpool.

Wright was probably the child of Edward Wright, a joiner of Edmund Street, who was born on 23 March 1723 and was baptised at St Nicholas's Church on 4 April. Alternatively, he might have been the son of Richard or William Wright, a bookbinder living off Old Hall Street. Wright was living in Old Hall Street when his son Edward was baptised at St Nicholas's on 10 April 1746, and when a daughter, Nancy, was also baptised there on 24 June 1748. On the first occasion he was described as 'painter' and on the second as 'limner'. He was recorded at the same address in the rate book of 1758. His neighbours included the portrait painter William Caddick (1719/20–1794) and the more famous George Stubbs (1724–1806).

Wright had almost certainly moved to London by 1761, when he accompanied the fleet sent to escort the future Queen Charlotte across the Channel, and from which he produced the painting *Princess Charlotte's Passage to England, September 1761* (NMM). In 1762 he was living in Craven Buildings, Craven Street, Strand in London, and he is also known to have lived in Pimlico. He was an active member of the Incorporated Society of Artists and exhibited there 1765–70. He also exhibited at the Society of Artists, 1762–67, and the Free Society, 1764. His painting *The Fishery* won a prize of 50 guineas from the Society of Arts for the best sea-piece in 1764 and he gained the same award again in 1766 and 1768.

Wright died around 1773, his death supposedly hastened by an unsuccessful exhibition in York and the premature death of his son Edward.

The only documented work to have been completed in Liverpool is a *View of St Nicholas Church and the Tower from Mann Island*, which was engraved by Clement and gives little flavour of Wright's style. All his known oils date from after his move to London. They include naval encounters, such as *The Battle of Quiberon Bay* (NMM) and *The Squadrons of Thurot and Elliott in Ramsey Bay* (Manx Museum), and storm and moonlight scenes. There are good examples of his work in NMM and WAG, which both have versions of *The Fishery*.

Lit.: *ODNB*; Bennett 1978: 236–37; Davidson 1986: 16–17; Wright et al. 2006: 848.

William G. Yorke (1817–1893)

William Gay Yorke was a Canadian-born carpenter and shipwright who became a marine artist after he settled in Liverpool in the mid-1850s. Although he seems to have achieved some success in the role, he moved to New York in the early 1870s, where he continued his artistic career, supported by his second wife Mary, until he died twenty years later.

Yorke was born in St John's, New Brunswick, Canada in 1817, the son of Thomas Yorke, who had settled there and became a carpenter after service in the province and in India as a corporal in the 25th Dragoon Guards. Nothing is known of young Yorke's Canadian upbringing, and he next enters the records when he married Susan Ball, the daughter of a Bristol painter, Joseph Ball, at St Martin's in the Fields Church in Liverpool on 7 April 1841. He gave his occupation as a carpenter, which could include working in the shipping industry, the same profession as his father. Their daughter Elizabeth Ann was born in the town in 1842, but by the time their two sons William and Edward were born in 1847 and 1852 respectively they were back in his native St John's. The reason for the move is not clear, but it might have been work- or family-related. Whatever the circumstances, they had returned to Liverpool by September 1856 when their youngest daughter, Susan Emma, was born in Toxteth.

Yorke seems to have begun his artistic career in the late 1850s, and his earliest surviving paintings date from this period. He is listed as a marine painter living at 2 Blythe Street, Everton, in *Gore's Directories* for 1860 and 1864. This is the same address given in the 1861 census when he was living there with his wife, two sons and a daughter. Yorke gave his occupation as 'marine painter' but an entry alongside adds 'ship wrt' – that is, shipwright. This would not be inconsistent with his declared status as a carpenter when he married and suggests that, at this stage, he was unable to sustain himself solely as a painter. It is unclear what family issues occurred in the following few years, but clearly by 1871 Yorke had separated from his wife and was living alone at 1 Sidley Street, Toxteth, accompanied only by a 21-year-old local servant girl, Margaret Angus. His occupation is given as marine artist. His wife and eldest son were living together at a separate address in Everton, although his youngest son, Edward, was working as a barman and living in a public house in St James Street, Liverpool.

Although he appears to have been building up a reasonable reputation and clientele in Liverpool providing ship portraits, Yorke moved to New York, probably in late 1872 or early 1873. There are paintings signed 'Lpool' in 1871 and 1872, indicating that he was still in the town for at least part of 1872. He is listed as an artist in the Brooklyn directories for three years from 1873/74 at 99 Prospect, 57 Fulton and Eagle, and then again in 1881 and 1882 at 96 Eagle. A large part of his output at this time was portraits of yachts and yachting scenes at the various races held around New York harbour. On 6 October 1880 Yorke married Mary E. Leidburg in Manhattan, conveniently forgetting that he had a wife in England (she lived until 1898), but no doubt working on the premise that no one would know. This also suggests that he had no contact with his family back in Liverpool. Mary assisted him with his painting, particularly after he sustained an injury in a boating accident in 1882 when he lost an eye, and she might even have been the major partner in these later years. They lived in a house in Brooklyn's Erie Basin and used a small boat as a floating studio.

Yorke died in The Refuge, Erie Basin Hospital, New York from pulmonary tuberculosis on 1 February 1893, and was buried in the Green-Wood cemetery in Brooklyn two days later.

Yorke's Liverpool period paintings are usually signed 'Wm York', generally with the addition 'Lpool' and a date, sometimes including the month. After his move to New York he seems to have used the signature 'Wm G Yorke' followed by the date. His portraits are usually quite lively, not only featuring the main vessel depicted but also other ships and boats in the distance, often shown in the Liverpool approaches or off the North Wales coast. He frequently shows the reflection of the bow in the water, and like a number of other artists he includes a seagull or two flying over the waves in the foreground. He occasionally portrayed a particular event, such as the capture of the British ship *Emily St. Pierre* by the Federal sloop *James Adger* off Charleston in March 1862.

W. G. Yorke, *Lord Palmerston*, signed and dated 1863, 64 x 92 cm. This is one of Yorke's standard profile portraits, completed whilst he was still resident in Liverpool. (New Brunswick Museum – Musée du Nouveau-Brunswick, http://www.nbm-nnb.ca, 1968.27)

There are no examples of his work in British public collections, but he is well represented in PEM, New Brunswick and Mystic Seaport, Connecticut.

Lit.: Davidson 1986: 91–98; Davidson 1995: 21; Finamore 1995: 63, 66; Falk 1999, III: 3665; Wright et al. 2006: 851.

William H. Yorke (1847–1921)

William Howard Yorke no doubt developed his artistic talents under the tutelage of his father William G. Yorke (q.v.), and he seems to have embarked upon a career as a marine artist at the earliest opportunity. He was probably the best-known and most prolific ship portraitist in Liverpool after the death of Samuel Walters in 1882, though his output virtually ceased after the turn of the century, whether through age, ill-health or the decline in popularity of ship portrait painting.

Yorke was born in St John's, New Brunswick, Canada on 4 November 1847, but the family had moved to Liverpool by the time his youngest sister, Susan Emma, was born in September 1856.[1] In 1861 he was 13 and was living with his family at 2 Blythe Street, Everton. By 1871 his parents had parted and Yorke was living with his mother and sister at 9 Sykes Street, Everton, and although only 23 was described as a marine painter.

He married his cousin, Lydia Phoebe Ball, the daughter of his mother's deceased brother Joseph, at St Barnabas's Church, South Kennington, Lambeth, on 21 September 1875, when he gave his occupation as marine artist, the son of William Gay Yorke, also a marine artist. They were living at 2 Isaac Street, Toxteth, when their son Percy was baptised at St Paul's, Princes Park, on 21 September 1876. In 1881 the family was still living in Isaac Street, and Yorke's younger brother, who was described as an unemployed public house manager, was living with them. Yorke was described as 'marine artist' and 'painter'. Whilst he was becoming a well-established artist at this time, his income was probably very modest, and his wife is listed in the local directory for the same year as a dressmaker in Molyneux Street. Her income probably made a significant difference to the family finances and continued over the following decades.

In 1891 the family moved to 93 Belgrave Road, a modest terraced house in Toxteth, and both his mother Susan, aged 75, and his mother-in-law and aunt Lydia Mary, now a widow of 59, were living with them.

They also had a 25-year-old commercial clerk, William Wilson, boarding with them. They were still living there in 1894, though they had moved next door to number 91 by 1900, according to local directories and the 1901 census. By this time their son Percy was working as a lithographic artist near Nottingham. On each occasion Yorke's occupation is given as marine artist.

He was an active member of the Liverpool Artists' Club, serving as vice-president for a number of years from 1894.[2] It also seems that he was something of a performer, because there are several references to him giving recitations at club events, including the dinners held for the hangers of the Autumn Exhibition.[3] His speech proposing the health of the press at a dinner in 1896 was remarked upon for its humour.[4]

By 1911 the couple had moved to a five-roomed house at 57 Lark Lane, and Yorke was again described as a marine artist–painter. His output had virtually ceased by this time, and he might have effectively retired, perhaps by choice or perhaps because he found it difficult to find commissions. The demand for ship portraits seems to have declined as the development of photography allowed quick, accurate and cheap representations to be produced, and the changing nature of seafaring increasingly saw the rise of larger shipping companies and less direct personal relationships between captains and ship owners and their vessels. Indeed, Yorke's wife might well have been the main breadwinner. She continued to run her own business, being listed as a linen draper and milliner further along Lark Lane at nos. 87–89 in the local directory in 1911. Yorke was still a well-known figure in artistic circles, and Davidson reports conversations with picture dealer Mr S. Davey and collector William Goffey, who both remembered him, the former commenting that he was a tall, pleasant gentleman who always wore a trilby hat.

Yorke died in June 1921 at the age of 73 and was buried in Allerton Cemetery. His wife survived him by more than twenty years, dying in Cheltenham in 1945.

1 His name is sometimes given as 'William Horde Yorke', but this is an error. His name appears in full as William Howard Yorke in several official documents, including when he signed the marriage register.

2 *Liverpool Mercury*, 21 December 1894.
3 There are several reports in the *Liverpool Mercury* in the early 1890s, e.g. 30 August 1894.
4 *Liverpool Mercury*, 20 January 1896.

W. H. Yorke, *Reliance*, signed and dated 1885, 63 x 95 cm. This portrait follows Yorke's standard practice of a port profile of the featured vessel filling the canvas with a familiar landmark in the background, in this case the coast of Anglesey. (NML/MMM)

The claim that Yorke completed a painting in 1858 at the age of 11 does not seem sustainable. It is more likely that he began producing works in his early twenties, and a painting of the *Ericsson* signed 'Wm H York Lpool 1869' is probably one of the earliest. Other early paintings are signed 'Wm H York' but from the mid-1870s he uses the signature 'Wm H Yorke' followed by the date, and usually includes 'Lpool', probably as an additional way of distinguishing him from his father. He ceased to add the reference to Liverpool after about 1890, perhaps when he knew his father had given up painting.

His portraits are competent but less imaginative than those of many of the artists of earlier decades. They generally adopt a standard pattern, with the ship, usually in a port profile, almost filling the canvas and any further detail such as another vessel or a familiar landmark or coastline very much in the far distance. The vast majority of his subjects are sailing vessels, normally under full sail, though he did occasionally paint steamers.

Yorke was obviously a conscientious and dedicated craftsman who often produced detailed drawings and sketches of the vessels he painted. In 1903 he made a scale model of the barque *Veronica* which was based on sketches he had made when the vessel was in port in 1883 and 1894. He used it to provide expert evidence in the trial of several seamen accused of murder on board the ship. A painting of the barque, dating from 1893, is now in the New Brunswick Museum.

NMM has more than a dozen works by Yorke and there are small collections in MMM, NMW and Grimsby, and in the US in PEM, Mystic Seaport, Connecticut, and New Brunswick Museum, Canada.

Lit.: Davidson 1986: 91–98; Davidson 1995: 21; Finamore 1995: 70, 72, 75, 77; Wright et al. 2006: 851; Tibbles 1999: 243–48.

APPENDIX

Possible Liverpool Marine Artists

There are a number of marine artists who have, or might have, worked in Liverpool. They include:

- those who claimed to be marine artists but to whom no works are attributed;
- established artists who produced an occasional marine-related work;
- artists who produced only one or two marine paintings with a probable, but unproved, Liverpool connection.

John Boydell (1838–1913)

John Boydell was a frame maker and picture dealer who also described himself as a marine artist on a number of occasions, though only one general landscape by him has come to light.

Boydell was born in Bedford, Leigh, Lancashire in 1839, the son of James Boydell, a silk weaver, and his wife Margaret, and he was baptised on 17 March. His father died the following year and in 1841 he was living with his mother, also a silk weaver, and his aunt in Chapel Lane, Leigh. His mother married Joseph Rimmer, another silk weaver, in 1849 and they were living in High Street, Bedford, Leigh. They were still there in 1851 when 12-year-old Boydell was working as an errand boy.

He had moved to Liverpool by the time he married Mary Leatherbarrow at St Joseph's Roman Catholic Church on 14 May 1860. Their first son, James Joseph, was just a month old when the 1861 census was taken and the family was living with Henry Collins, a cabinet maker, and his wife in Royden Street, Toxteth. His occupation is given, perhaps surprisingly, as railway stoker.

By 1871 they were living at 131 Great Howard Street and Boydell had clearly progressed. Not only did he have a growing family but he is listed as a 'marine artist' and they employed a young female domestic servant. They were still in Great Howard Street in 1881, and the family had grown again. They now had two sons and four daughters and he is described as a 'landscape artist'. James Joseph and his eldest daughter, Helena, were both at art school. During this period Boydell is listed regularly in the local directories, initially as a marine artist then in combination with picture framing, and in the last decade as an artist and art dealer. He is not listed after 1889.

In 1891 he was living in Moorfields with adjoining commercial premises and gave his occupation as picture frame maker. His youngest son, 19-year-old Frederick, was listed as a picture dealer. Charles Palin, a 23-year-old picture frame maker, was also lodging with the family.

His 'beloved wife' Mary died on Christmas Day 1891 and Boydell remarried in early 1893, taking Ann Jones as his wife. However, later in the decade he seems to have fallen on hard times, and in May 1899 a newspaper advertisement announced 'the disposal of the goodwill, fixtures and stock in trade of the old-established business carried on by Mr John Boydell of 51 Moorfields'.[1] Less than a month later, 'the valuable stock' of John Boydell 'picture and general art dealer' was offered for auction by George Gaunt, who was acting under a deed of assignment, a legal arrangement assigning the assets of an insolvent debtor to a trustee.[2] Two years later Boydell was clearly in straitened circumstances. Although he was still described as a picture painter, he and his wife were living in a court in Batchelor Street, just around the corner from Moorfields. By 1911 he was still described as an artist, but his wife had died and he was living with Stephen Smith, a dock labourer, and his wife in Sherlock Lane, Wallasey, on the Wirral. Boydell died, aged 76, in early 1913.

His eldest son, James Joseph, continued his artistic career, giving his profession as artist when he was admitted to the Liverpool Dramatic Lodge of the Freemasons in 1891, but again no paintings by him have surfaced.

It is difficult to know to what extent Boydell actually produced paintings, but an advertisement for a sale that he organised at his premises in Great Howard Street in 1884 included 250 oil paintings and watercolours 'principally by John Boydell whose reputation as a local artist has been considerably enhanced since successfully exhibiting at the autumn exhibition of last year'.[3] His only known painting is *The Lledr Valley near Betys-y-coed* in Manchester City Art Gallery.

Lit.: Davidson 1986: 107–09; Wright et al. 2006: 111.

1   *Liverpool Mercury*, 12 May 1899.
2   *Liverpool Mercury*, 6 June 1899.
3   *Liverpool Mercury*, 16 September 1884.

William Cleator (1815/16–1871)

This artist is known from a single entry in the 1853 edition of *Gore's Directory* where William Clator [*sic*] is listed as 'marine-portrait painter' living at 4 Water Street, Edge Hill. He worked as a house painter but probably had some artistic talent which he sought to develop. However, no examples of his work are known.

The 1851 census records William Cleaton [*sic*] living at 4 Water Street with his wife Mary and son John, who was two months old. The census gives his place of birth as the Isle of Man and tells us that he was a 35-year-old painter journeyman. They had sufficient means to employ a servant.

William Cleator was born in Ramsey, Isle of Man, to John and Mary Ann Cleator and was baptised on 4 February 1816. When he came to Liverpool is not clear and he is not identifiable in the 1841 census. When the 1861 census was taken the family was living at 44 Sun Street, Toxteth, and his wife is listed at that address, together with John and another son, Thomas, aged 8 months, and a daughter Ann, 8. The census helpfully tells us that her husband was in the Isle of Man and that he and another son, William, who was 5 years old, were staying with his sister Mary Skillhorn, a widow who was a smallware dealer. William senior's occupation is given as painter.

By 1871 tragedy seems to have struck the family. The census shows that William Cleator, painter, was a pauper in the Toxteth Workhouse. It seems likely that he had had a major stroke as he is described as 'dumb idiot'. He is still listed as married but his wife has not been traced. His sons John and William, who were lodging in nearby Lamport Street, had followed their father's occupation and were both listed as painters. William senior died in the workhouse later that year, aged 55.

Lit.: Davidson 1986: 128.

Frank T. Copnall (1870–1949)

Frank Thomas Copnall was a successful portrait painter who produced the occasional maritime painting, usually of a local Merseyside subject.

Copnall was born in Ryde on the Isle of Wight on 27 April 1870, the eldest son of Thomas Copnall, a grocer, and his wife Sarah. Copnall senior sold the business in July 1879 and in 1881 he was working as a provisions traveller, and he, his wife and seven children were living at 1 Romilly Road, Islington, London. They were sufficiently secure to employ a general servant, though Thomas seems to have encountered financial problems soon afterwards.[1] They moved to Merseyside and in 1891 they were living at 16 Edith Street, Poulton-cum-Seacombe. Copnall, now 20 years old, was working as a stationer, but it seems he had begun painting in his spare time. He exhibited a portrait at the Liverpool Autumn Exhibition for the first time in 1894. He seems to have combined his knowledge of stationery and painting when he applied for a patent for 'toned paper for artists' use' in 1895.[2] In the same year he completed his first portrait for the Liverpool Artists' Club, and the following year became an artist full-time.

Copnall was still living with his parents in 1901, at 42 Kenilworth Road, Poulton, and though he is listed with them in 1911 at 28 Faulkner Street, Liverpool, the local directory shows that he had his own premises at 2 Rock Street, New Brighton. He exhibited his first picture at the RA in 1902 and showed regularly both locally and across the country. He was a member of the Liverpool Academy, the Liverpool Sketching Club, the Artists' Club, of which he was sometime president, and the London Portrait Society. He maintained a studio at various locations in central Liverpool from 1900 until at least 1938.

On 1 February 1915 he married portrait and flower artist Theresa Nora Butchart (1882–1972) at St Margaret's Church in Toxteth. Earlier that week he had been presented with a Georgian tea and coffee service from his fellow members of the Artists' Club.[3] The couple spent some time at the artists' colony in St Ives before 1920.[4] At the time of the census in June 1921 Copnall was visiting Cardiff and his wife was at home at 4 Kings' Gap, Hoylake, with their three sons, the youngest of whom was only a few weeks old and was being looked after by a nurse. In September 1939 he and his wife were living at 26 Queen's Road, Hoylake, and one of their three sons, Andrew, an accounts clerk at ICI, was living with them. Copnall died on 13 March 1949 aged 78.

Frank Copnall was in constant demand as a portraitist and painted many of the leading people in the locality. In 1942 he reckoned to have painted over 1,000 portraits.[5] A handful of atmospheric and impressionistic maritime paintings by him survive, including a view of the Cunarder *Lusitania* off the Pier Head, dated 1909 (NMM), and two watercolours of local shipping and yachts racing in the Mersey. *Almost Home*, a sunset view off the coast dated to 1895, and a view of the Mersey during wartime with barrage balloons have passed through the market in recent years.

Lit.: Bennett 1978: 74–75; Davidson 1986: 129; Wright et al. 2006: 269.

---

1 *Liverpool Mercury*, 19 September 1883; *Morning Post*, 19 September 1883.
2 *Liverpool Mercury*, 22 February 1895.
3 *Liverpool Daily Post*, 30 January 1915.
4 Whybrow 1994: 216.
5 *Liverpool Echo*, 16 June 1942.

Frank T. Copnall, *View
of Liverpool from the Water*,
17 x 18 cm. This small,
atmospheric oil sketch is
in stark contrast to the
formal, academic portraits of
worthies which constituted
Copnall's usual output.
(Bonhams)

Joseph Desilva (1815/16–1883)

Joseph Desilva acted as an agent for a number of marine
artists, including McFarlane, Witham and Yorke. His
principal occupation was as a house painter and sup-
plier of paints and oils, though he was at times also an
outfitter and brass founder, and attempted to become a
licensed victualler. His painting business also supplied
artists' materials. The existence of one signed painting
suggests that he might have produced the occasional
ship portrait himself.

Desilva was born in Liverpool in 1815/16 to Manuel
de Silva, a Portuguese mariner who had settled in the
town, and his wife Anne, formerly Mitchell, a local
girl. He was baptised at St Peter's Church on 4 August
1817. The next we hear of him is as a painter, plumber
and glazier in 1841 when he was still living with his
widowed father and siblings in Thomas Street, but the

local directory records that he had a shop at 50 Waterloo
Road. Over the next forty years he had similar premises
at a number of locations in Liverpool. For many years
his principal works was in Bath Street, but in later life
he and his family lived on the Wirral.

Desilva married Martha Williams, the daughter of
a joiner, in January 1847, and by 1851 they were living
at his works in Bath Street and they had a young son
and daughter. He was doing well enough to employ a
17-year-old general servant. His occupation is listed
as 'outfitter', which usually refers to a seller of men's
clothes and uniforms, so perhaps he had expanded his
business and was supplying seafarers with their working apparel. He continues to be listed as a painter in the
local directories.

He has not been traced in the 1861 census, but
Martha had died by 1869 when he married Ann Jackson,

describing himself then as a brass founder.[1] By 1871 they were living in Regent Road with two teenage daughters and a teenage son, who was listed as an apprentice plumber. Desilva's own occupation is given as 'Master Painter, Plumber etc.' and he is similarly described in 1881, when he was employing four men. By this time, he and his wife were living in Liscard on the Wirral, and in the local directory he is listed as 'De Silva, Joseph Esq.' amongst the clergy, gentry and private residences. Business had presumably been very good for him.

However, there were clouds on the horizon and in December 1881 a notice appeared in the *Liverpool Mercury* announcing the sale on 10 January 1882 of 'the whole of the stock of oils, colours, varnishes, tools etc.' belonging to Mr Joseph Desilva at his premises in Bath Street, Liverpool. The reason given for the sale was that he was 'declining business on account of ill-health'.[2] Less than a month later his name appears in the bankruptcy lists as a defaulter at the stock exchange, indicating that there might have been other reasons for the sale.[3] It was clearly a time of worry and stress when perhaps he was searching for any way of recouping some of his financial losses, and in September he applied for a victualler's licence for his premises in Regent Road. When he was refused on the grounds that there were nine other licensed establishments within 170 yards, he protested, as the *Liverpool Mercury* describes it, 'excitedly shouting out that he was an Englishman and the Premier had said that no man could be condemned before he was heard', and later shouted, 'You may ruin me if you like.'[4]

In February 1883 he sold off the utensils and stock he had acquired for the victualling trade and at the end of April he was discharged from his bankruptcy.[5] After this period he makes no more public appearances, though further tragedy struck when his eldest son, also Joseph, died in Pennsylvania in 1888 at the age of 40.[6]

By 1891 Desilva and his wife were living at a less select address in Liscard, in Water Street, and though his fortunes might have improved somewhat – he is described as 'living on his own means' – they had taken in a boarder, a 34-year-old tobacconist's assistant. Desilva died in the spring of 1893 at the age of 75.

The suggestion that he might have been a marine artist originally came from the discovery of four unsigned watercolours of American ships in and around the Mersey, one of which bears a billhead for 'Josh De Silva, painter, plumber and glazier' of Bath Street made out to the 'Captain and owner of the ship Action Guard', and dated 25 September 1860. The same billhead also bears the tag 'Portraits of Ships taken in any situation … Specimens always on hand' and led to the conclusion that Desilva himself was the artist. Further investigation, however, showed that the composition of one of the watercolours is almost identical to a painting attributed to McFarlane, and with the discovery of other watercolours by McFarlane it seems that the whole group should be attributed to him.

It is worth noting that another painting of the American ship *Timor*, signed 'W. Yorke', also bears a pencil inscription on the frame, 'Joseph Desilva, 4 Regent Road, Liverpool'. A signed painting by McFarlane of the American ship *Ellen Austin* probably also had a Desilva trade label until it became detached.

In 1991 an oil painting of the steamer *Nyanza* which was signed 'J. Desilva 1872' appeared at auction. Whilst this provides evidence that Desilva was an artist in his own right, it is clear that his main activity was in selling rather than producing paintings. The 1882 sale of stock from his paint works included 'a number of valuable oil paintings, principally well-known ships trading in this port, and painted by Witham, York, McFarlane and others'.[7] And the sale in February 1883 included 'six oil paintings, marine subjects in gilt frames by local artists'.[8] Desilva was obviously an active dealer in the works of other marine artists.

Lit.: Davidson 1986: 84–86, 89; Davidson 1995: 22.

---

1   The Bath Street premises are listed as uninhabited, and 75/76 Regent Road is not included in the 1861 census.
2   *Liverpool Mercury*, 30 December 1881.
3   *Liverpool Mercury*, 28 January 1882.
4   *Liverpool Mercury*, 8 September 1882.
5   *Liverpool Mercury*, 27 February 1883, 23 April 1883.
6   *Liverpool Mercury*, 9 June 1888.

7   *Liverpool Mercury*, 30 December 1881.
8   *Liverpool Mercury*, 27 February 1883.

Thomas Dove Junior

An oil painting of the Inman liner *City of Paris*, signed and dated 'Thomas Dove junior / 1891', was noted by Davidson. There are two possible candidates who were related to Thomas Dove (q.v.) – his son Thomas (1837–1901) or his grandson, also Thomas (1867–1950).

The son was born in Liverpool in 1837 and baptised at St Peter's Church on 15 June that year. He was a ship's cook and was frequently away at sea. His only recorded voyage is on the *European*, serving as chief cook for a salary of £6 a month from 8 April 1870 until he was discharged on 21 May 1871. He married Mary Jane Burt, the daughter of a master mariner, at St Jude's Church, West Derby, on 10 September 1865. They were to have four sons and a daughter. In 1871 the family was living at 3 Mill Street and in 1881 they were at 8 Huskisson Street, Birkenhead. The family does not appear in the 1891 census, but by 1901 Mary Jane had died and Dove had retired from the sea. Two unmarried sons and an unmarried daughter were living with him. Dove died in the early summer that same year.

Grandson Thomas was born on 31 March 1867 and baptised at St Peter's, Liverpool, on 2 June. He was still at school in 1881 but has not been traced in the 1891 census.

He is listed in the local directories as a hairdresser in Bootle in the years from 1888 to 1894. In 1901 he was still living at home and is described as a 'hairdresser shopkeeper' working on his own account. His younger brother, Joseph, was almost certainly assisting him as he is listed as a 'hairdresser's assistant'. Dove married Charlotte Mary Usher on 8 October 1901. By 1911 they had a son, Thomas Aaron, aged 8, and a daughter, Grace Elizabeth, 4, and were living in Rock Cottage, Castle Street, Caergwrle. However, Dove seems to have changed professions because he is listed as a photographer working on his own account. How successful this change of career was is not clear, and the next reference in the 1939 census describes him in his original profession of hairdresser. He and Charlotte and Thomas Aaron were still living in Castle Street, Caergwrle. He died there, aged 83, on 23 June 1950, leaving £177 to his widow.

There is a slight preference for identifying the artist as the grandson – the signature of the son on his marriage certificate is very crude and not something one would expect from someone with artistic dexterity. The grandson's interest in photography perhaps indicates an artistic leaning and an interest in composition.

Lit.: Davidson 1986: 130.

J. A. Drinkwater (active c. 1970–c. 1995)

A number of ship portraits in oil and watercolour dating from the 1970s through to the 1990s by this Liverpool-based artist have appeared on the market, but nothing has been found to identify the painter.

Peter Ghent (1855–1911)

Peter Ghent was a talented landscape artist and watercolourist, who produced an occasional painting that qualifies as a maritime subject.

Ghent was born in Congleton in March 1855 to Peter Ghent, a ham dresser and game dealer, and his wife Elizabeth.[1] He was not baptised until 16 March 1860, when the service took place at St Peter's in Congleton. By 1871 the family had moved to Birkenhead and was living in Chester Street, where Peter senior had set himself up as a hairdresser. Ghent initially worked in his father's barber's shop but also studied at the Birkenhead School of Art, where he came under the influence of John Bentley, the head of the school. He married Harriet Mary Hatton at St John's Church, Liscard, on 6 October 1876.

---

1   The name is spelt as 'Gent' in early references, including the 1861 and 1871 censuses, but the artist always used 'Ghent' in adult life.

Peter Ghent, *Burning of the Liverpool Landing Stage*, signed, 31 x 62 cm. The destruction of the landing stage by fire in 1874 was painted by several artists, but this is one of the most dramatic accounts. (WmAG)

Ghent began exhibiting at the Liverpool Autumn Exhibition in 1877 where his work immediately drew considerable praise. He attracted the attention of Alderman Edward Samuelson, chairman of the Arts Committee, and several of his works were bought for the permanent collection of WAG. He and his growing family had moved to Llanbedr in North Wales by the time of the census in 1881, and he was working as a full-time landscape artist, exhibiting at all the major exhibitions throughout the country. He exhibited at the RA 1879–96, at Suffolk Street, Royal Institute of Painters in Watercolours, the Royal Institute of Oil Painters, the Royal Society of Arts, Birmingham, Manchester, Dudley and the Royal Cambrian Society, of which he was a founder member in 1881.

Ghent was still in Llanbedr in 1891 and his family had grown to a son and six daughters, and they were able to employ a general servant. By 1901 they had moved to Llanrhos, near Conway, and the family had grown by a further son and daughter. Philip Osment (q.v.) was staying with them at this time.

However, it seems that Ghent's later years did not live up to the promise of his youth. As his obituarist wrote, 'adverse conditions clouded his later years; he ceased to exhibit and he passed more or less from memory'.[1] Why this should have been is unclear, though the obituary also refers to a 'long distressing illness'. Ghent had moved to Liverpool by 1904, living at 131 Grove Street, where he died on 19 February 1911. He was buried in Toxteth Cemetery on 22 February.

Ghent was highly regarded as a young landscape artist, being picked out for special mention on a number of occasions and eliciting the view that 'his genius as a watercolourist shone resplendently at one period in his life'.[2] His marine subjects include an accomplished and atmospheric rendering of the burning of the Liverpool landing stage, which took place in 1874 (WmAG) and which he might well have witnessed. Two fishing views have also recently passed through the auction rooms in Canada.

Lit.: Bennett 1978: 103; Wood 1978; Wright et al. 2006: 362.

---

1   *Liverpool Daily Post*, 21 February 1911.
2   Ibid.

E. L. Greaves (active 1860–1880/85)

E. L. Greaves is known from a number of rather stylised watercolour portraits, and a Liverpool connection has been suggested because many of the vessels depicted are registered or associated with the port, and they often feature a Liverpool pilot schooner in the background. Additionally, one painting has a label on the rear for 'E Whitnall, Fine Art Gallery, 45 Castle Street, Liverpool', which was in business from 1873 to 1884.

Davidson suggested quite reasonably that he might have been E. Greaves, a mariner, who appears three times in the Liverpool directories, in 1868 at 4 Beaufort Street, in 1875 at 27 Brighton Terrace, both in Toxteth, and in 1880 at 17 Olivia Street, Bootle. However, no references to either E. L. Greaves or E. Greaves can be found in the usual sources, and this might substantiate the view that he was a seafarer. Given that many of the paintings are now in Canada and that several of them are of vessels registered in Yarmouth or New Brunswick, a Canadian connection, or even origin, is also possible. In the absence of other information, it might be best to assume that he was a part-time artist, with some maritime background, who spent at least part of his adult life in Liverpool.

The surviving portraits all follow a similar format of a sailing vessel in a port profile at sea, often with a Liverpool pilot boat in the background, and usually with an inscription in pen and ink under the portrait identifying the vessel, its home port and its master, referred to as 'commander'. Most are signed but only one is dated, *Missouri + Liverpool H A Calhoun Commander* (New Brunswick Museum, Canada), to 1860. Most of the other vessels were in service for a number of years in the period 1860–90, and with information about the master several are likely to date from the early 1870s.

The New Brunswick Museum hold four examples, the Yarmouth Maritime Museum two, and a further half dozen or so have appeared on the market in the last thirty years.

Lit.: Davidson 1986: 130.

J. H. Harrison (active c. 1880–1890)

Davidson includes a reference to this artist as a resident of Runcorn and had seen a well-executed watercolour of the barque *Naiad*. They were probably an amateur/part-time artist but unfortunately with such a common name it has not been possible to discover any further information about them.

Lit.: Davidson 1986: 131.

Isaac Heard (1804–1869)

Isaac was the younger brother of Joseph Heard, and though generally listed as a portrait painter, it is possible that he occasionally assisted his elder sibling with some of his ship portraits.

Heard was born at Egremont on 14 March 1804 and was baptised two days later. Nothing is known of his early life, but he exhibited portraits in Whitehaven in 1826 and Carlisle in 1827. The local paper commented on the excellence of the resemblance of the early portrait and thought it was 'highly creditable to his abilities'.[1] On the first occasion he gave an address in London and on

---

1   *Cumberland Pacquet and Ware's Whitehaven Advertiser*, 8 September 1826.

the second addresses in both London and Whitehaven. It may be that he was trying his luck in the capital, but certainly by 1834 he was living and working in Liverpool, when he is first listed in the local directory.

In 1841 he was living in Toxteth, with a 7-year-old daughter, Margaret, and a female servant, but the lack of any mention of his wife suggests he was a widower. Ten years later the census shows he had remarried, and though he himself was staying with his widowed aunt Jane Heard, in Queen Street, Whitehaven, his wife Margaret, aged 42, and his daughter, now a dressmaker, were both living in the family home in Toxteth. In 1861 they were living in Salisbury Street, West Derby, and they had a son, also Isaac, aged 6. His daughter by his first marriage was also still living with them. In both these later censuses, his occupation is given as portrait painter.

Isaac Heard died from debility and chronic cystitis on 20 October 1869 at 43 Priory Grove, Everton, aged 65.

Heard is referred to as a portrait painter in the censuses and the local directories from 1834 to 1849. Although on one occasion he is referred to as a marine painter, no examples have come to light and it seems likely that the names and specialisms of the two brothers were confused. The two brothers were clearly close, sharing the same trade address in the local directories for more than a decade, though maintaining separate personal households. How well Isaac fared as a painter in his own right is open to question – only one signed portrait by him has been located, suggesting that he was perhaps less successful than his older brother. The possibility remains that at slack periods he helped Joseph out with his ship portraits.

Lit.: Davidson 1986: 51.

H. Hutchinson (active c. 1870)

This is another artist included by Davidson for 'a good quality oil painting of the Harrison line vessel *Statesman*' off Port Lynas, but no further work has come to light, and again it has not been possible to discover any further biographical information.

Lit.: Davidson 1986: 131.

Richard Jenkinson (1787–1828)

Richard Jenkinson was the son of John Jenkinson (q.v.) and was a painter. He almost certainly exhibited some marine-related views at the Liverpool Academy, though no paintings are currently known.

Jenkinson was born in Liverpool on 8 May 1787, the son of John and Esther Jenkinson, and was baptised at St Nicholas's Church on 22 June. He was probably the R. Jenkinson who exhibited four paintings, three of them entitled *View of the North Shore* (which almost certainly included some shipping), at the Liverpool Academy in the same years that his father was also an exhibitor.

Jenkinson was described as 'painter' when he married Julia Clinch at St Anne's Church on 17 April 1817. They were probably living in his father's former house at 14 Russell Street in 1821, though the directory gives his name as Robert, presumably a misprint. When their daughter Esther was baptised in July 1826, he was living in Union Street and he is again described as a 'painter'. On this occasion his wife's name is given as Juliet. He died less than two years later, and was buried at St Paul's Church on 16 January 1828, aged 40. He was still living in Union Street.

Lit.: Davidson 1986: 28; Morris and Roberts 1998: 350.

T. Hampson Jones (1846–1916)

Thomas Hampson Jones was a Liverpool-born landscape artist who worked mainly in watercolour and produced the occasional marine-related painting.

Jones was born in Everton in 1846.[1] Despite his unusual middle name, it has not been possible to trace any official records until the last decade of his life. He became a well-respected artist and there are regular references in the local press, mainly to works of his appearing in local and national exhibitions. He exhibited at the Liverpool Autumn Exhibitions from the late 1870s until just before the First World War, and at the Liverpool Society of Watercolour Painters, of which he was president in 1890 and 1891.[2] He had 24 works shown at the RA between 1876 and 1903, and also exhibited at the Grosvenor Gallery and the New Watercolour Society.

Jones appears in a number of local directories with a studio in Union Buildings, Cook Street, in Liverpool from at least 1894 until his death. He seems to have been based in Birkenhead for most of his later life but he was also a frequent traveller. He was 'still in Venice' in March 1882 when he sent two watercolours to the RA and his obituary comments that he 'travelled a good deal', including visiting Italy, India, Ceylon and Burma.[3]

In 1911 he was living as a boarder with Alice Ellen Wilson, a widow, and her family at 31 Balfour Road, Birkenhead. He was still there when he died on 26 November 1916. He had never married and probate was granted to Mrs Wilson and a solicitor for the sum of £274. A sale of his watercolours and paintings by other artists, including William J. J. C. Bond and David Cox, took place in September 1917.[4] A portrait of the artist by William Logsdail (1859–1944) is in WAG.

Jones was principally a landscape painter, 'in which he showed much delicacy of touch and boldness of conception'.[5] He occasionally chose a marine-related subject, such as his Venetian scenes of 1882, *Hay Barges off a Quay*, dated 1879, or *A Calm Evening on the Medway*, exhibited in 1881. He painted some scenes around the docks in Liverpool and Davidson illustrated a drawing of a becalmed sailing ship.

Lit.: Davidson 1986: 131, 139.

1   His obituary in the *Liverpool Daily Post*, 29 November 1916, and his entries in the death and probate registers all state that he was aged 70.
2   *Liverpool Mercury*, 3 April 1890, 19 January 1891.
3   *Liverpool Mercury*, 27 March 1882; *Liverpool Daily Post*, 29 November 1916.
4   *Liverpool Daily Post*, 18 September 1917.
5   *Liverpool Daily Post*, 29 November 1916.

H. MacLeod (active c. 1850–c. 1870)

This artist is known for a painting of the Rock Ferry paddle steamer *Sylph* signed and dated 1851 (MMM), and Davidson notes a collector in New York having seen other paintings signed 'H McLeod Liverpool', though none have recently been located. He was almost certainly a part-time or amateur artist. He could possibly have been 35-year-old Greenock-born Hugh McLeod, who was living at 21 Kent Terrace, East Kent Street, Liverpool in 1851. He was listed as 'painter', though this probably means that he was a house or ship painter rather than an artist. He had a wife, Catherine, 35, born in the Highlands, and a 6-year-old daughter, Christina. No other information about him or his family has been found.

Lit.: Davidson 1986: 133; Tibbles 1999: 158–59; Wright et al. 2006: 547.

J. McAlister (active c. 1855–1860)

J. McAlister is only known from two oil paintings on oval glass panels – a view of Rock Ferry with the PS *Wasp* and a view of the Liverpool waterfront from Rock Ferry, both in WmAG. The panels seem to date from about 1855–60 and are topographically accurate, the view of Liverpool being particularly detailed and featuring the wealth of activity on the river, including a large sailing ship and a variety of small boats and river craft. It has been suggested that they were originally part of the decoration of one of the Rock Ferry boats.

Unfortunately, with no corroborative information it has proved impossible to identify the artist.

J. McAlister, *Liverpool from Rock Ferry*, signed with address, c. 1855, 32 x 49 cm. This unusual glass painting and its companion are the only known works by this artist. (WmAG)

James Moughtin (1818–after 1877)

Davidson noted a painting of the iron paddle steamer *Douglas II* by J. Moughtin and suggested that the artist might have been be shipwright James Moughtin. Further research suggests that he is still the most likely candidate, but no further works are known.

James Arthur Moughtin, the son of James Moughtin, a miller, and Anne (née Caine), was born at Jurby on the Isle of Man, and baptised on 17 September 1818. His occupation was given as shipwright when he married Sarah Johnson, the daughter of a cheesemaker, at St Bride's Church, Liverpool, on 22 May 1845. In 1851 they were living in Mill Street, Toxteth, with a daughter, Mary Ann, aged 3, and a son, William, aged 1. Their eldest son James, born in 1846, is not included and he might have been with relatives. They cannot be traced in the 1861 census, but Moughtin is listed as a shipwright

at 24 Alder Street, Toxteth, in the local directories from 1867 to 1873 and then at different addresses until 1877.

The only other census entry is for 1871, which gives the Alder Street address and confirms that he was 52 and was born in Jurby, Isle of Man. Sarah was 44 and they had two children living at home, Frederick, 19, a stonemason, and a daughter, Sarah, aged 9. His wife Sarah probably died in 1884 but further details of Moughtin himself have not been traced.

His eldest son, also James, could possibly be the artist. He was baptised on 29 November 1846 in St Bride's Church. He became a boot and shoemaker and married Sarah Ann Haigh, the daughter of a shipwright. They had a number of children and were living in Wolfe Street in 1881 and Tamworth Street in 1892. He died in November 1892, aged 46.

Lit.: Davidson 1986: 134.

W. Pike (active c. 1835–c. 1845)

Pike is known for a small number of well-portrayed portraits of vessels, usually against a detailed Liverpool-related view, suggesting that he might have had a maritime background and have been based in the port.

There were a number of William Pikes in Liverpool around the time of the dated paintings, including a carter and a glassworker, but Davidson's suggestion that he should be identified as William Pike, a master mariner, listed in the 1827 directory as living in Gerard Street, behind Shaw's Brow, seems plausible. This would seem to be the William Pike who was born about 1804 and married Jane Tait at St Peter's Church in March 1821, and then Ruth Danold in the same church in September 1830, Jane presumably having died in the intervening period. They had a son, William Danold Pike, who is listed twice in the bishop's transcripts of baptisms, in November 1835, when they were living in Duke Street, and in March the following year, when they were in Park Lane. It has not been possible to trace the family after this date with any certainty, either in Liverpool or elsewhere, though a William Pike from Liverpool, of approximately the right age, is listed amongst British seamen in the period 1841–44 and in 1853.

Known paintings include a profile of the brigantine *Albion Entering the Mersey*, with the Perch Rock fort and lighthouse in the distance, signed and dated 'W. Pike / 1839'. A portrait of the snow *Cybele*, similarly signed and dated 1835, shows a wider view of the Cheshire side of the Mersey, including the Perch Rock fort and lighthouse, the entrance to Wallasey Pool and the lighthouses, flagpoles and windmill on Bidston Hill. As Davidson comments, the degree of detail supports a familiarity with the Mersey estuary. Interestingly, Samuel Walters (q.v.) owned a painting by Pike, which was included in the studio sale after his death.[1]

Lit.: Davidson 1986: 135–36.

1 No details given other than the name 'W. Pike', *Liverpool Mercury*, 26 May 1882.

George Sampson Reynolds (1803–1888)

George Sampson Reynolds was a full-time artist, who produced portraits, animal paintings and genre pieces.

Reynolds was born in Plymouth in 1803, the son of Richard Reynolds, an army officer, and his wife Hannah, and was baptised at Stoke Damerel Church on 23 January. He seems to have spent much of his early life abroad, judging by an advertisement for lessons which he placed in the latter years of his life, 'having studied upwards of twenty years on the continent, in Rome, Venice, Munich, Brussels, Antwerp &c.'. He also 'exhibited in the Royal Academy and other exhibitions in London'.[2]

Reynolds is first traceable in the censuses in 1861 when he was lodging in Hamilton Square, Birkenhead, at the home of Patrick Waldron, a master bootmaker, and his wife. He was unmarried and described as 'artist, portrait and animal'. He married 49-year-old Elizabeth Ker Grimes, the daughter of John Grimes, Controller of Customs at Liverpool, on 20 April 1870 at St John's Church, Birkenhead. Just over twelve months later they were living at 6 King Street, Birkenhead, and were employing a cook.

By the time of the 1881 census they had moved to Ryde on the Isle of Wight, where they were living at Northampton Villa in Pellhurst Road. Reynolds is listed as an artist and his wife as an annuitant, thus in receipt of a private income. He was listed in *Kelly's Directory* as an artist at that address in 1885, and he died there on 10 January 1888, leaving under £100 to his widow.

Davidson notes a painting of the Liverpool waterfront with well-executed detail, but no other marine subjects have been found.

2 *Isle of Wight Observer*, 22 January 1881.

Lit.: Davidson 1986: 136; Wright et al. 2006: 668.

J. Sanders (active 1875)

Davidson noted and illustrated a painting of the barque *Dartmouth* inward bound off Anglesey, signed J. Sanders. He suggested that the artist might have been James Sanders, a dock master from Trafalgar Dock, or John Sanders, a paint manufacturer, painter and plumber of Bridgewater Street. With only the one painting it is impossible to know if there is a Liverpool connection or to identify the artist with any degree of certainty.

Lit.: Davidson 1986: 136–37.

Leonard Sharpe (1894–1979)

Leonard Sharpe is best known as the author of two of the *How to Draw* series of books, one devoted to merchant ships and the other to the Royal Navy. They were first published in 1945 and 1950 respectively but were popular throughout the 1950s. He lived in Liverpool and Bootle from the late 1920s until his death.

Davidson first established a Liverpool connection from local artistic contacts and confirmed that Sharpe was a freelance commercial artist who lived in Merton Road, Bootle, for a number of years. He undertook commissions for the Cunard and Blue Funnel lines, as well as producing occasional ship paintings. Davidson recorded that he was remembered as a kind and gentle man who always bought his materials from Wilson's Bookshop in Church Alley, just off Church Street.

It seems that he was born William Leonard Sharpe in London in March 1894, the son of Thomas Sharpe, a clerk and later an accountant, and his wife Ada.[1] The family was living in Charlton, South London, in 1901. His mother died in 1905 and his father remarried a couple of years later. By 1911 they were living at 122 Heathwood Gardens, Old Charlton, and Sharpe was an apprentice electrical engineer. He married Margaret Garvey in Newcastle-upon-Tyne in the autumn of 1917, and they were living there when their first four children were born between 1918 and 1923. They had moved to Liverpool by the time their last child was born in 1929.

In September 1939 Margaret and the family were living at 79 Sedgemoor Road in north Liverpool, but Sharpe was staying at 17 Baucher Drive, Bootle, and gave his occupation as 'Advertising manager/mechanical draughtsman'. He was clearly using his artistic talents for commercial purposes and had produced several books on the subject, including *The Artist in Commerce*, published in 1936, *Some Business Hints for the Commercial Artist*, 1938, and *The Technique and Practice of Advertising Art* which he co-authored in 1939. He was living at 37 Pembroke Road, Bootle, when he died on 24 April 1979, and probate was granted the following year for just over £12,000.

Apart from his books, very little of his work is known, but Davidson illustrates a painting of the Blue Funnel Line's *Alcinous*, which is signed and dated 1961.

Lit.: Davidson 1986: 136.

---

1   Various dates are given for his birth – 2 March, when he was baptised in 1910; 3 March in the 1939 register; and 4 March in the index of the register of deaths.

Frederick Shaw (1847–1923)

Frederick Shaw was a lithographic artist who also produced watercolours, mainly of landscape and genre subjects. His only marine-related works are a small number of evocative dockside sketches of Liverpool.

Shaw was born in the summer of 1847 to William Shaw, an engraver, and his wife Jane. Shaw lived at home at various addresses in Everton until he married in about 1874. In 1881 he was living with his wife Mary and their growing family at 36 Burleigh Road, Everton, and was described as 'lithographic writer and artist'. They had moved to 27 Royal Street, Kirkdale, by 1891 and he was still living there in 1894, according to *Kelly's Directory*, and had a studio at 22 North John Street, which he maintained until at least 1900.

By 1901 he and his family had moved to 60 St Domingo Vale, which was to be his home for the rest of his life. He described himself on this occasion as 'artist, painter and designer', though he uses the term 'lithographic artist' again in 1911 and 1921. Shaw died on 2 May 1923, and probate for his estate of £610 was granted to his widow.

Shaw was a founder member of the Liverpool Amateur Sketching Club from 1872. His neat and attractive watercolours, with titles such as *River Crossing and Cattle*, *The Letter*, and *On the Marsh, Formby*, occasionally come on the market.

Lit.: Davidson 1986: 137.

G. W. Stevens (active c. 1870–c. 1890)

G. W. Stevens was responsible for a group of naive but attractive watercolours which generally feature small tugs, paddle steamers and ferries, against an accurate topographical background, usually off the Liverpool waterfront or one of the landing stages on the Wirral side of the river.

The attribution to Stevens is based on *A View of the Seacombe Ferry Stage* in MMM, which is signed and dated 'G W Stevens 1888'. All other known examples are unsigned but are clearly by the same hand.

All attempts to identify Stevens have proved unsuccessful.

Lit.: Davidson 1986: 109–10.

G. W. Stevens *The Old Seacombe Ferry Stage*, 34 x 63 cm. Stevens is known for a number of similar naive views of locations along the Mersey and one or two other local marine paintings. (Bonhams)

BIBLIOGRAPHY

Anonymous (1959), *Exhibition of Works by Samuel Walters (1811–1882)* (exh. cat.), Bootle Art Gallery, 6 April–2 May 1959.

Bennett, Mary (1978), *Merseyside Painters, People and Places: Catalogue of Oil Paintings, Walker Art Gallery, Liverpool*, Liverpool.

Brewington, Dorothy E. (1981), *Marine Paintings and Drawings in Mystic Seaport Museum*, Mystic, CT.

Brewington, M. V., and Dorothy Brewington (1981 [1968]), *Marine Paintings and Drawings in the Peabody Museum*, Salem, MA, rev. ed.

Burleigh, J. C. P. (1991), 'Joseph Parry, Artist: Dates and Origins', *Transactions of the Historic Society of Lancashire and Cheshire*, 140, 229–32.

Davidson, A. S. (1986), *Marine Art and Liverpool: Painters, Places and Flag Codes, 1760–1960*, Wolverhampton.

Davidson, A. S. (1992), *Samuel Walters – Marine Artist: Fifty Years of Sea, Sail and Steam*, Upton, Wirral.

Davidson, A. S. (1995), 'Across the Western Ocean: American Ships by Liverpool Artists', in Finamore 1995, 9–26.

Davidson, A. S. (2001), *Marine Art and the Clyde: 100 Years of Sea, Sail and Steam*, Upton, Wirral.

Davidson, A. S., and Anthony Tibbles (1999), *Marine Art and Liverpool – A Postscript: Fifty Ship Paintings by Francis Hustwick (1797–1865)*, Upton, Wirral.

Davies, Peter (1992), *Liverpool Seen: Post-war Artists on Merseyside*, Bristol.

Falk, Peter Hastings (1999), *Who Was Who in American Art: 400 Years of Artists in America*, 2nd ed., 3 vols, Madison, CT.

Finamore, Daniel (1995), *Across the Western Ocean: American Ships by Liverpool Artists*, Salem, MA.

Hay, D. (1979), *Whitehaven: An Illustrated History*, Whitehaven.

Lee, Sidney (ed.) (1900), *Dictionary of National Biography*, London.

Martin, Kenneth R. (1992), *The Maritime Folk Art of A. De Clerck*, Bath, ME.

Morris, Edward, and Emma Roberts (1998), *The Liverpool Academy and Other Exhibitions of Contemporary Art in Liverpool, 1774–1867*, Liverpool.

Oliver, Charles W. (1993), 'Harry Hoodless ARCA ATD FRSA', in *Harry Hoodless, A Retrospective Exhibition* (exh. cat.), Williamson Art Gallery, 13 June–11 July 1993.

Read, Gordon, and Michael Stammers (1994), *Guide to the Records of Merseyside Maritime Museum*, 1, St John's, Newfoundland.

Rideout, Edna (1927), 'The Cheshire Companies and Old Quay', *Transactions of the Historic Society of Lancashire and Cheshire*, 79, 148–74.

Rubinstein, William D., Michael A. Jolles and Hilary L. Rubinstein (2011), *Palgrave Dictionary of Anglo-Jewish History*, London.

Tibbles, Anthony (1999), *Illustrated Catalogue of Paintings: Merseyside Maritime Museum, Liverpool*, Liverpool.

Tibbles, Anthony (2007), 'Portraits: Ships', in John B. Hattendorf (ed.), *Oxford Encyclopedia of Maritime History*, Oxford University Press, III, 319–26.

Watney, Bernard (1993), 'William Jackson of Liverpool', *Transactions of the English Ceramic Circle*, 15.1, 122–33.

Whybrow, Marion (1994), *St Ives, 1883–1993: Portrait of An Art Colony*, Woodbridge.

Williams, Gomer (2004 [1897]), *History of the Liverpool Privateers and Letters of Marque with a History of the Slave Trade 1744–1812*, Liverpool.

Wilmerding, John (1971), *Robert Salmon: Painter of Ship & Shore*, Salem, MA.

Wood, Christopher (1978), *Dictionary of Victorian Artists*, Woodbridge.

Wright, Christopher, with Catherine Gordon and Mary Peskett Smith (2006), *British and Irish Paintings in Public Collections*, New Haven, CT.

Websites

Oxford Dictionary of National Biography, www.oxforddnb.com

http://atlantic-cable.com/Books/1857Isaac/index.htm

https://www.oxfordartonline.com/benezit